SIGNED WITH THEIR HONOUR

SIGNED WITH THEIR HONOUR

THE STORY OF CHIVALRY IN AIR WARFARE 1914-45

PIET HEIN MEIJERING

MAINSTREAM
PUBLISHING

First published in 1987 by
MAINSTREAM PUBLISHING COMPANY
(EDINBURGH), LTD.
7 Albany.Street
Edinburgh EH1 3UG

ISBN 1 85158 063 8

British Library Cataloguing in Publication Data
Meijering, Piet Hein
   Signed with their honour : chivalry in air warfare.
   1. Air warfare——History
   I. Title
   358.4′009′04   UG625

   ISBN 0-85158-063-8

Front cover painting by Serge Stone
Cover design by James Hutcheson

Typeset in 11 point Times by Pulse Origination, Edinburgh.
Printed by Biddles Ltd., Guildford, U.K.

Contents

List of Illustrations

Foreword

THAT the author has asked me to write a foreword to his book, even though when he and I were young men our countries were on opposite sides of a terrible war, is indicative of the spirit of goodwill in which it was written. This spirit was evident to me when I got to know Mr Meijering personally and was reading his manuscript.

I think that, besides being a man of wide reading and moral philosophy, the author needed to have a lot of courage to work out the theme of chivalry in the air war into a publication. Because the air wars are chiefly — and by most people exclusively — remembered for their inhuman aspects.

In 1912 the Chief of Staff of the French Army made the remarkable statement that the aeroplane might be an excellent tool for sporting activities, but could never be used for military operations. Unfortunately, he was wrong!

In fact it all started in World War I, with unarmed, underpowered wooden and linen flying machines, flown by brave aviators, exchanging salutes when they occasionally encountered the enemy in the air, and developed into serious combat, in which just one fact became important: "either you or me". This was the time when chivalry could come up. It should be taken into consideration, however, that some of those actions may have been prompted by little more than a sense of fairness. As the author points out, fairness is one of the basic elements of chivalry.

It was quite different in World War II, because of the more advanced technology and the fact that strategic bombing soon

9

became the most important use of the air forces. The strategic plans and objectives came to include civil targets and consequently the civilian population. Under these circumstances, heroism and unselfish sacrifice were still to be found, as in any war, but of course chivalry got the worst of it. That the author has nevertheless been able to find some examples of chivalry in the air war at that late stage is something to be thankful for.

However, as Mr Meijering repeatedly stresses, any positive side-effects of war, such as chivalrous behaviour, may never be an excuse for justifying or glorifying war. This would be reprehensible in regard to any war, but emphatically so when we think of the horrors of the whole- and self-destroying inferno of a nuclear war: the ultimate capital crime.

Regrettably, fighting, combat and war are still in existence and seemingly ineradicable. But strong powers are making serious efforts to banish war from the earth. Let us work and pray that they are successful.

What we owe to the author is that he has painstakingly collected instances of chivalry in the earlier air wars, and can now show us that there have been recent times when noble behaviour was not unknown between men fighting each other. Even if this should never happen again in war, the same kind of behaviour in peacetime could indeed raise the tone of society and might give peace initiatives more chance of success.

Having read Mr Meijering's manuscript several times with great interest, I should be surprised if a great many readers were not as captivated by the subject and the way it is treated as I was. My best wishes for the success of this book accompany its publication.

Adolf Galland

Author's Preface

AS far as I can recall, I was 16 years of age when I first read Ernst Udet's autobiography *Mein Fliegerleben*. He was one of the best-known pilots in World War I, in fact the most successful German fighter pilot who survived the war.

I was then — as I have remained for the rest of my life — an aviation enthusiast, and Udet's book, telling of his adventurous life in war and peace, fascinated me. The episode that made the strongest impression on me was his encounter with the famous French top ace, Georges Guynemer, who was so chivalrous as to refuse to shoot down and kill Udet when he saw that the German was no longer able to defend himself. I have retold this incident to introduce the first chapter of my book.

In the years that followed, avidly reading everything on the war in the air I could lay my hands on, I came across a surprising number of other instances of chivalrous behaviour. They delighted me. Apparently the age of chivalry was not past! I started making notes of everything I found on the subject, though I did not have any definite object in mind yet. As a matter of fact I did not understand very much of chivalry. It was all very gallant, thrilling and romantic, but the essence escaped me. What was the underlying element of human nature that accounted for both chivalrous behaviour and people's admiration for it?

To me, enlightenment came with the reading of *Homo Ludens: A Study of the Play-Element in Culture* by the famous Dutch historian, Johan Huizinga (1872-1945). In it he presented

11

his notion of play as an essential factor in human civilization, coming to the conclusion that

> real civilization cannot exist in the absence of a certain play-element, for civilization presupposes limitation and mastery of the self, the ability not to confuse its own tendencies with the ultimate and highest goal, but to understand that it is enclosed within certain bounds freely accepted. Civilization will, in a sense, always be played according to certain rules, and true civilization will always demand fair play. Fair play is nothing less than good faith expressed in play terms.*

From then on I began making plans to work my notes into a book. I soon realized, however, that I would not have the time to complete it before I had retired from my professional work (which had no relation at all to aviation, nor with the writing of history). In the meantime I could do little more than use the material I had gathered from books and articles to make out a draft. Later I would add to that by delving into official archives in several countries and interviewing people who by their experiences in the air war might be able to contribute valuable items.

But now that I am retired I find that I still have not got sufficient time, nor the means, to cover the subject as thoroughly as I had intended. Rather than letting all my work and thoughts on the subject go to waste, I decided to finish the book anyway, with published sources as the only explanatory material. While fully conscious of the shortcomings of this procedure, I nevertheless trust (with not too much vanity, I hope) that my study of chivalry in the air war will be of interest to a specific audience, and contribute to a better understanding of much that has often been disposed of as sentimental nonsense. Actually I am rather surprised that the subject has not been treated systematically much earlier. A great many writers have touched upon it, but always as incidental to their main theme.

Writing about chivalry, I had to guard constantly against letting myself be carried away by the glamour of the subject and against being uncritical of my sources. In an amused sort of way I could envy Winston Churchill who, writing about the Arthurian legend, could take the view he expressed in that

* Huizinga, *op. cit.,* p. 211.

Guynemer

delightful sentence: "It is all true, or it ought to be; and more and better besides."* It is a viewpoint that obviously does not befit a writer dealing with a 20th-century phenomenon. Still, it seems in many cases to have been held by authors of books on the First World War, when describing the noble and glorious

* Winston S. Churchill, *A History of the English-Speaking Peoples* Vol.I (1956), p. 47.

13

deeds of the heroes in the air. I do hope I have been able in all cases to sift the wheat from the chaff.

I think I owe the readers an explanation as to why I have not written this book in my native language, Dutch. I had three reasons for this, two having to do with the natural wish of an author to be read by as many people as possible.

In the first place, for reasons I will not go into here (as far as I know them!), the Dutch are in general much less receptive than the English-speaking peoples to any facts and ideas about warfare that by any stretch of the imagination could be construed as putting war in a favourable light. It is as if they do not want to be told of heroism, chivalry, unselfish sacrifices and adventures in war, for fear of losing sight of the fact that war has become the most horrible experience mankind can go through. It seems they cannot objectively observe those positive elements that are part of it as well, and find some solace in them.

My second reason was simply that there are far more people in the world who can read English than there are who understand Dutch.

Lastly, nearly all the quotations I wanted to use were in English. By writing in English myself (which was not particularly difficult — I used to teach it) there was no need to translate them, which always detracts from the value of texts. It saved a lot of work, too, of course.

I wish to acknowledge my debt to all the authors whose books and articles have provided me with the material necessary to my own treatise. Their names and the titles of their publications will be found in the notes at the back of this book. I am particularly indebted to J. M. Spaight, *Air Power and War Rights* (3rd ed., 1947). Not only did the text of this book supply a wealth of information, the references in the footnotes to a great many books I had not even known the existence of were most helpful and time-saving to me.

I am much obliged to Dr. I. H. Ph. Diederiks-Verschoor, emeritus Professor of Air Law in the University of Utrecht. Her early interest in my plans for this book was a welcome stimulant for me to develop them further.

My friends Harry van Asten and Jan Ipema were kind enough to read the typescript critically. They came up with quite a few useful comments and suggestions. I am grateful for the time they devoted to this. I also thank Jan Ipema for helping me to find the answers to a few small problems concerning German matters, and for parting so generously with Gottschalk's rare book on Oswald Boelcke.

P. H. Meijering
Utrecht
The Netherlands

1

A revival of chivalry

ONE early morning in June 1917, Ernst Udet, a German fighter pilot, had reached a height of 5,000 metres after taking off from his base in the Champagne region of France. He flew alone. The *Jagdstaffel* he belonged to, *Jasta 15*, had only four aeroplanes at their disposal for the time being, and they were not able to do much more than fly the required patrols singly. Udet was 21 and not very experienced yet, though he had already shot down six enemy aircraft and could be called an "ace", if one followed the French custom in this matter.

It was his plan this day to make an attempt to shoot down one of the string of observation balloons on the French sector of the Western Front. But, looking down and around, orienting himself, he presently saw another aircraft approaching from the west and flying at the same height. He was soon able to identify it as a French SPAD 7, also a single-seater. Udet sat up and prepared himself for the inevitable man-to-man battle.

Soon the two adversaries were flying in tight circles, each trying to get into a position on the other's tail, so that he could use his machine-guns, which could only be fired straight ahead. The aircraft were so near to one another that Udet could distinguish the narrow, pale face in the leather helmet of the Frenchman. On the fuselage some words were painted. It was only after circling for some time that Udet was able to make out the word *Vieux*. This came as a shock, for it was common knowledge among the flyers at the front that *Capitaine* Georges Guynemer, the famous French fighter pilot, had *Vieux Charles* painted on the aircraft he flew. This must be

17

Two famous German fighter pilots of World War I, in 1918, each wearing the Pour le Mérite: *Ernst Udet (right) and Eduard Ritter von Schleich. Both survived the war. Galland says of von Schleich: "He was a gentleman of the old school, perhaps too much so for the grim business at hand."* (IWM)

Guynemer, Udet thought, the greatest of all enemy pilots, the man who had 30 victories to his name. Only last month he had witnessed Guynemer shoot down his friend "Puz" Hänisch.

Udet fully realized that he did not stand much chance of surviving this duel, the less so because Guynemer flew a plane that was superior to his. Not only was his Albatros much slower and unable to climb as fast, it also had a nasty habit of shedding its wings in a dive.

Udet flew with all the skill he could muster, but it was a hopeless fight. He had already taken some hits in his aircraft but he fought on, trying all the tricks, none of which could fool the great master. Then, incredibly, for a fleeting moment, the SPAD flew across Udet's sights. He pressed the gun button . . . but nothing happened. Both guns were jammed. Still flying in circles, Udet hammered with his right fist on the breeches of the guns. This primitive remedy sometimes

18

worked. Then he used both fists. Suddenly Guynemer, flying on his back, sped across Udet's line of flight, apparently observing what his adversary was doing. Once again he swept past Udet. This time he waved, then dived westwards towards his own lines.

Eight minutes this duel had lasted, the longest minutes in Udet's young life. Bewildered, Udet flew home. He knew that Guynemer could easily have shot him down, but that he had not wanted to kill a helpless foe. It would have been beneath his dignity.

There are those, Udet has written, who say that Guynemer's guns must have jammed too, that he was not able to fire either. Others have speculated that Guynemer may have been afraid that Udet, in desperation, would try to ram him. "But I do not believe them. I think that even today there is still alive something of the knightly heroism of olden times. And that is why I lay this belated wreath on Guynemer's unknown grave."[1]

What Guynemer did can be regarded as the supreme act of chivalry: sparing in combat the life of a helpless enemy who has not surrendered.[2] Such an act was not as common in the air wars as some romantic writers will have us believe. Still, it has not been difficult to find more examples, some of which I shall present later on in this chapter and in chapter 3. Indeed, after delving into uncounted histories, biographies and memoirs, I am inclined to suppose that there would have been more instances of such noble gestures if there had been more opportunities for them. This supposition is founded on the fact that there were so many other, "lesser", manifestations of the chivalric spirit, and on the realization that opportunities were truly scarce. Not only would the pilot, in the heat of battle, have to notice signs that his adversary was defenceless, he would also have to decide that his helplessness was real, that it was not a ruse. This could well have to be a split-second decision, quite possibly with his own life at stake.

It is intriguing that chivalrous behaviour occurred at all in a 20th-century war, long after the age of chivalry was gone. Yet, indisputably, there was a revival of chivalry in the 1914-1918 air war. Contemporary writers and later historians and chroniclers agree on this almost unanimously, most of them

19

Georges Guynemer standing by his SPAD VII. He had the name Vieux Charles *(Old Charles) painted on the aeroplanes he flew, part of which is visible on the fuselage side.*   *(IWM)*

adding that the same cannot be said of the fighting on land and sea.

Lord French, who commanded the British Expeditionary Forces in France and Belgium in 1914/15, wrote:

> It is satisfactory to know that some such kindly and chivalrous spirit has at least made itself felt at times between the opposing flying services in the present war, for I have heard authentic stories which go to show this has been the case.[3]

An American (then neutral) war correspondent, who had talked with German flying officers, noted that

> only among the aviators of the fighting armies is one certain to find that chivalry which once was never dissociated from war. Theirs is the special heritage of preserving the knightly tradition. The extraordinary bitterness of the other arms of the service makes the contrast all the sharper.[4]

Another American correspondent, working among the Allied troops, wrote:

> It has repeatedly been said that in this war the spirit of chivalry does not exist, and, so far as the land forces are concerned, this is largely true. But chivalry still exists among the fighters of the air.[5]

Admiral Mark Kerr's opinion was that

> In the other elements chivalry almost disappeared on the side of the Hun, but in the air he actually was the starter of those exchanges of courtesy which became general in the fighting in Europe.[6]

In his memoirs covering the Battle of the Somme and Paschendaele, with their senseless mass slaughter in the sickening circumstances of trench warfare at its worst, Willie Fry, a fighter pilot, wrote:

> The public at home, and to a certain extent the ground troops in France, could not understand that, from the first, fighting in the air was conducted on chivalrous lines and not with the hate largely generated by propaganda, justifiably in order to keep up the tempo of the war effort.[7]

There is a danger that, after reading these and many other

testimonies, we tend to forget that chivalrous behaviour among airmen in the First World War, if not exceptional, certainly was not the rule. As an American writer says, "moments of chivalry and humanity stand out against the background of the war like poppies against the muddy fields of Flanders".[8] Chivalry was a sublimating, never a dominating factor in air warfare.

As the war progressed, the air forces of the belligerents expanded, and the aeroplane was used for more tasks than in the beginning. All this made the war in the air a much less individual affair. There were fewer chances for certain manifestations of chivalry, though others — as we shall see — continued as before. Also, the mood changed, from viewing the fighting with that fantastic new weapon as a highly adventurous and gentlemanly sport to a bitter and sometimes vengeful one. Pilots had seen friends die a horrible death in a burning machine from which they could not escape otherwise than by jumping to their deaths without a parachute (as some did). They had been witness to some merciless, vicious conduct by the enemy, which engendered real hate for him and a wish to avenge their friends. The elation of the first years gave place to a more realistic outlook, such as the viewpoint that sparing the life of an enemy meant that he lived to fight another day and that on that day he might kill your best friend, or yourself for that matter.

For all that, chivalrous behaviour did not disappear from the scene. What is more, it was observed again in the Second World War, at least in some theatres of war. Not only were there many gratifying examples of chivalry, the lack of it was condemned. Both combatants and civilians were shocked when they witnessed or heard of unchivalrous behaviour, even though the enemy who was "guilty" of it was often perfectly within his rights according to international law or usage. A notable example of this is the shooting at parachuting airmen who were going down over their own territory. This particular case will be treated at great length in chapter 3.

Is there an explanation for the revival of chivalry with the coming of the war in the air? I think there is, even a plausible one. The circumstances were extremely favourable to such a revival.

To begin with, even if chivalry had all but disappeared from warfare, the *interest* in it had not died with it. The romance of medieval chivalry had been kept alive in epic and song. The heroic exploits and honourable deportment of the knights "in shining armour" had not ceased to appeal to generations of men. In the early air war the pilots were all young men, some of them no more than boys, a few in their late teens.[9] At an impressionable age they got the opportunity to follow in the steps of the magnificent medieval knights they had heard and read about. What had not happened for centuries (except for incidental cases) now came true. Combatants went into battle like the mounted warriors (or *chevaliers*) of olden times. Their charger was not a living horse but a machine, yet alive with vibrating power, obeying its rider. In the clear skies — not contaminated with the mud, the filth, the ruins, the stench of death of the ugly battlefields below, where mass killing went on — they met the flyers of the other side as individuals, often in single encounters. Even when more aeroplanes were involved, combat was on a small scale. The pilots could identify themselves with the medieval knights, jousting or participating in tournaments.

Moreover, there certainly was a strong bond that united the flyers of all nations. Like the medieval knights, they belonged to a small, international brotherhood. They were the few who had learned to master that new and wonderful invention, the aeroplane. Wonderful and dangerous. There is a story that in the early days of the First World War messages were dropped by German flyers on French airfields, saying that it was useless to fight each other; there were enough dangers in the air without that![10] Others, no doubt, enjoyed the danger. Through the ages risking one's life has been part of the attraction of some sports. These men, in some cases knowing each other from pre-war meetings, now met as champions of opposing sides in a war. But the bond remained. It was a case of "we few, we happy few, we band of brothers", albeit on different sides of an unhappy conflict. A war correspondent put it like this:

> There is a freemasonry of the air. Some kind of affinity seems to exist between those who have taken to themselves wings to explore the vastness of space. It has survived the

23

snapping of all the other ties that once united us with our present foe. German airmen who rejoice in the slaughter of civilians from the skies show themselves of punctilious chivalry toward their foemen in space [. . .] The Royal Flying Corps on its side were equally courteous.[11]

Possibly there are other, minor, influences that helped chivalry to make a come-back. To me it is incomprehensible, however, that it has been argued that the new *machine*, the aeroplane ("this last and most ominous triumph of machinery"), was

an influence making for the revival of a spirit which is the very antithesis of all things mechanical. Romance and chivalry seem to have nothing in common with that doubly mechanical and coldy inhuman engine of war — a machine that flies carrying a machine that kills. Yet, strangely, the effect of the use of aircraft in war was at first to restore to warfare something of the spirit which went out with the Middle Ages.[12]

True, the writer speaks of *an* influence but, as he does not mention any other, we may assume that what he meant was that this machine was the principal one.

It was only natural that before long the fliers were compared with knights. David Lloyd George, Prime Minister of Great Britain, said: "They [the pilots of the RFC and RNAS] are the knighthood of this war, without fear and without reproach: they recall the legendary days of chivalry, not merely by the daring of their exploits but by the nobility of their spirit." In the literature of the 1914-18 war one quite frequently finds the pilots, especially the fighter pilots, referred to as "knights". I have seen at least four books with the title *Knight(s) of the Air*.

The fighter pilots of the Second World War in their turn were familiar with the heroic deeds of their predecessors in the First World War. No doubt for many of them their choice to become a pilot was influenced by the glamour that radiated from names like Ball, von Richthofen, Guynemer, Boelcke, Nungesser, Rickenbacker, and so many other aces. The Germans kept the memory of some of their greatest aces alive by naming units after them. After Oswald Boelcke's death on 28 October 1916 *Jasta 2*, which he commanded at the time, was by Imperial Decree named *Jasta Boelcke*. The name was also used in World War II but, strangely enough, for a bomber unit, *Kampfgeschwader 27*. A month after Manfred von Richthofen was killed on 21 April 1918, his *Jagdgeschwader Nr.1* was redesignated to *Jagdgeschwader Freiherr von Richthofen Nr.1*. At the instigation of Göring, who wanted to link his new Luftwaffe with the traditions of the 1914-18 war, Hitler signed a special order on 14 March 1935 to form *Jagdgeschwader Richthofen Nr.2*. When Ernst Udet, who was Germany's most successful ace to survive the First World War, died on 17 November 1941 the *Führer* gave his name to *Jagdgeschwader 3*. That Udet had committed suicide was, of course, kept a secret.[13]

It is difficult to say how strong the influence was of the accounts of the air-fighting in the First World War on the mentality of the pilots fighting in the Second. Probably it was a very real one on those who had learned to fly before the war, and a negligible one on pilots who were turned out by the war training programmes, with the attendant propaganda element. One of the old hands, *Oberstleutnant* Eduard Neumann, *Kommodore* of *Jagdgeschwader 27* in 1942-3, said after the war that

> It may be a little difficult for most people to understand today that the British flyers always enjoyed our respect and sympathy. This is more conceivable if one knows that in all German pilots' messes in peace time the old veterans of World War One always spoke of the British pilots, of air combat with them, and of the British fairness in the most positive way.[14]

When, with some satisfaction, we are able to record several instances of chivalrous behaviour in the Second World War, we have to acknowledge that it was very much less in evidence than in the First. In fact, it was non-existent in the war the Germans fought against Soviet Russia and in the Allied war against Japan.

With few exceptions, chivalry seems to have been confined to those theatres of war where the British and German air forces fought each other. Time and again we find evidence that there was between the German and British airmen a certain sympathetic relationship and understanding which, if not totally lacking, was rare between airmen of any other two nations at war with each other.

Erich Rudorffer, one of Germany's greatest fighter pilots in the Second World War, had something to say about this in an interview round about 1970. After relating how he had once been shocked to see a German pilot who had baled out of his Me 262 fighter being shot at by American P-51s, he said: "In the fighter war against Britain I had never seen this and in Africa I never saw it." He continued:

> It was different in the Battle of Britain. Once — I think it was 31 August 1940 — I was in a fight with four Hurricanes over Dover. I was back over the Channel when I saw another Hurricane coming from Calais, trailing white smoke, obviously in a bad way. I flew up alongside him and escorted him all the way to England and then waved good-bye. A few weeks later the same thing happened to me. That would never have happened in Russia — never.[15]

But even there where German and British airmen were each other's opponents in the air, the ever greater numbers of aircraft participating in the fighting, their ever greater speeds and the more sophisticated armaments that came to be used did away with many of the conditions conducive to chivalry.

Having postulated that chivalry did play an interesting part in the air wars, and having put forward an explanation of the unexpected re-emergence of a spirit that seemed to belong to a long-lost past, I shall in later chapters describe and illustrate various manifestations of modern chivalry in war. But first it is necessary to answer a few pertinent questions: What exactly is meant and implied by "chivalry"? What is its appeal? What are its origins?

2
The nature of a noble tradition

TO begin with, how should chivalry be defined? It is never easy to give an indisputable definition of an abstract notion. But to define chivalry is very difficult indeed, because it is a comprehensive idea, with several facets of unequal importance (or even of different meaning) to different writers. I need not make an attempt at it, however, for in this book I am expressly concerned with one particular aspect of chivalry, which I shall lead up to in the course of a brief characterization of chivalry in general and shall then define.

Chivalry can be broadly described as "the way the medieval knights were expected to live", the word also being used to indicate the knightly class or order itself.[1] As such, chivalry* was a European concept, originating in the 11th century in France, from where it spread over western Europe.

Some of its elements, however, are by no means typically European; nor did they come into the world for the first time in the Middle Ages. In fact, one basic element may be found in civilizations all over the world and through the ages. It is the play-element, which is fundamental to the notion of war as a noble game of honour. Now, like all games, the martial game was regulated by a collection of rules, a code of behaviour. This behaviour is itself often called chivalry. It can be defined as: "Behaviour in combat which is in accordance with a code of values, the foremost of which are honour, courtesy and fairness; with ritual and romantic overtones, and in any case an

* From the old French *chevalerie* — horsemanship, knighthood.

element of play." In the present book I shall use "chivalry" in this limited sense.

It was the Dutch historian, Johan Huizinga, who, in his *Homo Ludens: A Study of the Play-Element in Culture*[2], argued convincingly that play is "a distinct and highly important factor in the world's life and doings" and "that civilization arises and unfolds in and as play". He devotes a separate chapter to "Play and War", in which he states that "indeed, all fighting that is bound by rules bears the formal characteristics of play by that very limitation". The rules limit the degree of violence, but Huizinga stresses that "the limits of licit violence do not necessarily stop at the spilling of blood or even at killing".[3]

One can indeed go further and say that the very danger, the risk of death, makes combat — in particular individual combat — the most intense form of play, an exhilarating sport which men (or rather a certain class of men) have pursued from time immemorial. We see the same lure of dangerous adventure at work in several non-martial sports and activities today; motor racing, mountaineering and certain circus acts are obvious examples. They attract men not in spite of the mortal dangers but because of them.

Another interesting observation Huizinga makes is that war loses its play-quality when it "is waged outside the sphere of equals, against groups not recognized as human beings and thus deprived of human rights — barbarians, devils, heathens, heretics and 'lesser breeds without the law' ". In such circumstances war "can only remain within the bounds of civilization in so far as the parties to it accept certain limitations for the sake of their own honour".[4]

That the notion of war as a noble game, as the supreme sport, is almost gone now, is not because in a modern war combatants get killed in far greater numbers, but because of the *way* they die (and millions of non-combatants with them): in a war that leaves hardly any room for individual combat, a dehumanized, total war, which (in the words of Huizinga) "banish[es] war's cultural function and extinguish[es] the last vestige of the play-element".[5]

Today, the idea of war as a sport is apt to be considered absurd or even obscene. The memory of two world wars, with their massacres and other horrors and cruelties, and the constant threat of a third global war, which would inevitably end in a nuclear holocaust, have in most people evoked an aversion to war that is too strong to admit of any association with anything noble or playful. In earlier centuries such associations were quite natural. Then, when warfare changed, becoming a more impersonal and nationalistic concern, the play-element lost ground and chivalry declined. Its ideals, notions and customs became outmoded. Not in the sense that later generations found them hard to understand, or pathetic or even ridiculous. Only in the practical sense that their observance was — with rare exceptions — something of the past.

But it was a well-remembered past, stories of which were handed down from generation to generation (and embellished in the process). It was a heritage that appealed to a great many people. They experienced a vicarious satisfaction when reading or listening to narratives of the glorious deeds of the knights in their colourful and impressive garb, who fought in tournaments and jousts as well as in war with such admirable courage, courtesy and fairness, and regarded all those contests as noble games of honour.

These narratives idealized fact, and much of their content was heroic and romantic fiction. Even so, they had great influence. They conditioned combatants in later conflicts and wars so that they did not lose sight of the play element of combat, and might wish to conform to chivalry's ideals, thereby sustaining that influence. Thus, smouldering under the surface of harsh reality, there have ever been traces of the play-element in combat.

Huizinga was too pessimistic: not even in the two world wars in our 20th century was the last vestige of the play-element extinguished. On the contrary, as we have seen in chapter 1, the introduction of the aeroplane in warfare appears to have brought about a revival of chivalry, chiefly because the new weapon restored individual combat and gave rein to those intrepid young men who were eager to wage war as a game again. They played the game according to the traditional rules of chivalry, though not always interpreting them in the same manner. They knew perfectly well that these rules were not in any way official, but that hardly mattered to them. They felt them to be morally binding. They "thought then in terms of 'chivalrous obligation, the things that matter more than death' ".[6] They were of course also bound by official, legal rules, the international law of war. This was to them no problem at all, for the rules of chivalry set much stricter limits to violence, required far more restraint from the fighting men than international law did.

Few of the 20th-century combatants who set store by chivalrous behaviour will have been aware that French chivalry, in particular the experience of the joust and the tournament*, had served as a basis for international law. Certain practices which developed in jousting and tourneying evolved into rules that curbed the ferocity of the martial sports. Later these civilised conventions were also observed on the field of battle. "The knights of the 12th century had conducted their martial games like battles — their descendants made their battles resemble tourneys."[7] Later still, many of those rules found their way into the articles of international law.

> A whole series of conventions, whose purposes later genera-
> tions would rationalise into the framework of a nascent
> international law of war, can be seen achieving a measure at
> least of recognition in the 12th and 13th centuries, largely
> under the aegis of tourneying experience. It could indeed be
> argued that the relatively subtle influence of the tournament
> did more, in the long run, to promote standards of civilised
> behaviour between belligerent forces than papal prohibitions,
> issued in the name of restraining undisciplined violence, ever
> looked like doing.[8]

Huizinga goes farther back in time, beyond the classical to a purely archaic past. To the sacred origin: the primeval initiation rites, which "the tournaments and joustings, the orders, the vows, the dubbings are all vestiges of", and in all of which "the play-factor is powerfully operative and a really creative force". He does admit that "the links in this long chain of development are lost to us". But there is no doubt about the last link: "chivalry was one of the great stimulants of medieval

---

* A joust was a combat in the lists between two knights; a tournament was a fight between two groups of knights and their footmen, covering a wide area, ranging over the countryside and into villages. One can say that the joust was a mock duel and the tournament a mock battle.

civilization, and however constantly the ideal was belied in reality it served as a basis for international law, which is one of the indispensable safeguards for the community of mankind".[9]

Thus chivalry exerted its beneficial influence on modern warfare through two separate channels, of narration and of legislation.

Not surprisingly, history teaches us that the play-element in culture has not always and everywhere been strong enough to have an appreciable effect on the way wars were fought. Nor are we surprised to learn that, when it did have such influence, this did not result in uniform sets of rules of combat in each civilization. Nevertheless, one often wonders at great similarities between them, for example between the ethical code that governed warfare in ancient China, many centuries BC, and that of the European Middle Ages. On the other hand, one is sometimes struck by conduct so different from what one considers normal from the viewpoint of one's own culture that it is almost inconceivable. A good illustration of this is an episode from what is known as the Khalkhin-Gol or Nomonhan Incident, a short and undeclared Russo-Japanese war in 1939. On 7 August of that year a Japanese pilot, Daisuke Kanbara, shot down an enemy aircraft on the border of Manchuria and Mongolia. He watched the pilot of the disabled plane make a crash landing and struggle out of his machine. Whereupon he landed alongside his opponent and killed him with a traditional Samurai sword that he carried in his cockpit.

This raises the question of whether it is the vast difference in culture which existed between Japan and the Western countries that accounts for the absence of chivalry from the war these nations fought from 1941 to 1945.

This difference was without doubt the main cause. To explain further it is necessary to have a short look at the structure and spirit of Japanese society at the outbreak of the war. In no other 20th-century power was society such a strange combination of modern and ancient elements. The country had a modern industry, which had helped to develop a well-equipped and most efficient army and navy. But its religious and social ideas went back to ancient times, always under the strong influence of militarism, a consequence of the constant local wars that had afflicted the country throughout its history.

31

In fact, the military establishment, extreme in their views, regarding war and conquest as the highest good, dominated the country and easily suppressed any timid efforts to accept Western ideas and to promote peace. This created a highly dangerous martial atmosphere, especially in connection with the Shinto belief in the divine origin of the Japanese people, which led to the arrogant idea of national superiority, of being a chosen people, predestined to dominate the world.

The backbone of the Japanese military spirit was *bushido*. This was the traditional code of ethics of the *Samurai*, the knights of feudal times (12th-19th centuries). For centuries *bushido** was only followed by the *Samurai*. But when in the second half of the 19th century the country was opened to Western influence and the creation of a new Japan began, the modern armed forces incorporated the ancient code in their ideology and regulations. And although by the time the Second World War broke out more than half of the Japanese officers came from the lower middle class, their adherence to *bushido* was not in any way less than that of the descendants of the *Samurai*.

Bushido has been compared with the chivalric code of the European medieval knights. And, indeed, there are distinct similarities, such as the insistence on honour, loyalty and courage. But in one respect there was a great difference. Courtesy, an essential principle of European chivalry, was lacking in *bushido*. That is to say, courtesy in the sense of considerate behaviour towards one's foe, not in the sense of formal politeness, expressed in bows and the like, which may be nothing but empty gestures. On the other hand, one of the important elements of *bushido*, contempt for death, is not quite in keeping with the European chivalric conventions. Admittedly, there are many cases on record in which Western knights (medieval and modern) showed an awesome readiness on occasion to lay down their lives for the good cause or to save their comrades, or simply to exemplify the attitude that "life is nothing much to lose". But the Western fighter did not go to the extremes the Japanese did. To the Japanese being

---

* The term *bushido* (Way of the Warrior) was rarely used by the warriors themselves. It seems rather to have been coined at the turn of the 20th century.   (*Encyclopedia Americana*)

defeated, and especially becoming a prisoner-of-war, meant a fate worse than death. By surrendering to the enemy he brought the utmost disgrace upon himself, which is why the Allies took hardly any prisoners in the Pacific war. In hopeless situations the Japanese preferred to commit suicide.

All this goes far towards explaining why there was no chivalry in the war against Japan. When the Japanese went to war in December 1941, aggressively determined to achieve domination of the whole of East Asia and if possible the world, their immediate and spectacular military successes vindicated to themselves their inbred feeling of superiority. Their Western enemies were evidently inferior, both in military equipment and in mentality. More often than not they surrendered as soon as defeat had become inevitable, instead of fighting to the last man. This made them contemptible in the eyes of the Japanese. The contempt was not counteracted by any considerateness, and easily led to brutalities and cruelties towards helpless adversaries and even prisoners. Because in their view they were not dealing with equals but with lower beings, harsh treatment did not soil their honour, no more than ill-treating animals would do. If the Japanese were at all bothered by the fact that by abusing and even murdering prisoners they violated the international Prisoners of War Convention, 1929, it did not show. Although Japan was a contracting partner to this and other Conventions regarding warfare, those in power in Japan chose to ignore them, no doubt rating them less highly than Japan's divine mission to establish a New Order in Greater East Asia. Having started the hostilities without first declaring war, they subsequently rode roughshod over most international rules of warfare.

When we now look at the same war from the viewpoint of the Western nations, we come upon the irony that they, too, looked upon their enemies with contempt and did not regard them as equals either. Partly responsible for this was racial prejudice, which, by the way, led to a foolish disregard of a number of timely warnings that the weapons the Japanese had developed were at least as good as those of the West, and that the quality of their fighting men — also of their airmen — was excellent. But the Western nations had a far stronger (and legitimate) reason for their contempt, directly the war began. Japan's treacherous attack on Pearl Harbor without a declaration of war was a flagrant breach of international law. 7 December 1941 truly was "a date which will live in infamy", as President Roosevelt said on the following day.[10] In the years that followed the Japanese kept making a mockery of the international conventions, so that, quite understandably, the Western allies considered themselves at war with a morally inferior enemy, hardly recognized as human beings, "a lesser breed without the Law". In the chronicles of such a war one must not expect to find any trace of the play element, or any instance of chivalry.

The other theatre of war where chivalry was absent was Eastern Europe, where Germany invaded the Soviet Union in 1941 and after a grim and most bloody campaign was driven back to within Berlin in 1945. Here moral contempt for the enemy definitely played a part as well, on either side. But there was an additional factor, of a political nature.

As a general rule, the political system of a particular nation and its policy lie outside the immediate sphere of combat. This was even the case with Nazi Germany. The German armed forces fought under the flag with the *Hakenkreuz* — the swastika. This emblem of the National Socialist Party figured on their uniforms and on their Iron Cross and most other decorations; all German aircraft had swastikas painted on their tails. But, especially in the navy and the air force, only a small percentage of the fighting men saw themselves as champions of the National Socialist cause. The great majority fought for their country, right or wrong.

In the USSR this was systematically different. The Communist Party exercised firm control on the armed forces, on all levels. Ubiquitous political officers saw to it that the impact of party indoctrination did not weaken. If necessary they resorted to coercion.[11] True to Stalin's word that "he who cannot hate cannot fight", real hatred for the enemy was considered essential for a good fighting morale. It was therefore inculcated upon the Soviet soldiers, sailors and airmen. That it was sometimes necessary for the political commissars to take care that the hatred did not flag, can be gathered from stories of German pilots who were taken prisoner by the Soviets. They tell us of cases in which they had fairly normal human contacts with the Russian pilots they met and were able to talk frankly with them as long as the political officer was not present. Once they were sent on their way to a POW camp, their lot was a wretched one. Especially in the first two years their prospects were so dreadful that not infrequently German pilots who had come down in Soviet-held territory shot themselves or resisted capture in such a way that they were certain to be killed, rather than go into Soviet captivity.

The Russians on their part had every reason to fear being captured by the Germans, who at times grossly violated the Prisoners of War Convention, although their maltreatment of military prisoners was nothing to — and also unrelated to — the horrible crimes perpetrated in their concentration camps.

It stands to reason that in such circumstances chivalry had no chance at all.

There is something else that may have contributed to the absence of chivalry in the 1941-1945 Russo-German war in the air. During the first two years of the war Soviet fighter pilots laboured under a profound sense of inferiority toward the Luftwaffe.[12] No wonder. The Soviet Air Force (*Voyenno-vozdushnyye sily:* VVS) had suffered appalling losses in the summer of 1941. In the first week of the campaign, which began on 22 June 1941, more than 4,000 of their aircraft were lost, as against only 150 of the Germans. Two months later the Soviet losses had mounted to 7,500! The VVS had been deeply humiliated in combat with the Germans, who were superior in every military respect: organisation, equipment, aircrew training, combat experience and tactics.

Huizinga's remark that war loses its play quality when it is waged outside the sphere of equals refers to situations in which the one party considers itself *morally* superior to the other. One wonders, though, if the same may not also be true in case of an enormous *military* disparity, such as existed between the Luftwaffe and the VVS in 1941 and 1942, and if it may not then be the inferior instead of the superior party which is liable to scorn the humanizing elements of warfare.

It is of interest to note that the treatment of prisoners-of-war by the Soviets improved round about May 1943,[13] at a time when it was becoming increasingly clear that the tide of the war in Russia had turned. In the air war, too, the situation had improved considerably for the Russians. At Stalingrad the VVS had played a major role in deciding the outcome of the battle, and in the large air battles over the Kuban bridgehead in the Caucasus in April-May 1943 the Soviet Air Force clearly demonstrated that it had, in an incredibly short time, made a remarkable recovery from the disasters of 1941 and had become a proficient and highly dangerous adversary.[14] The VVS had risen like a phoenix from its ashes, more powerful than ever. It cannot be said that the sense of inferiority was completely gone now, but there was much more self-confidence.

We can do no more than speculate about a possible connection between the improvement in the treatment of prisoners and the lessening of the military inferiority of the Soviets.

In the next part of this book I shall deal with and give examples of the several ways in which chivalry has manifested itself in the air wars.

3

The quality of mercy

TO a chivalrous man, the killing of a helpless enemy is repugnant, incompatible with the ethics of a world he wants to live in, conflicting with the rules of civilised warfare as he knows them. What are his feelings when confronted with the opportunity — perhaps even the temptation — to kill a defenceless foe? I do not think I have ever seen them better described than by Charles Lindbergh (of Atlantic crossing fame), telling of an experience he had in the Second World War. Though he was a civilian then,[1] he flew some 50 combat missions in the Pacific theatre of war. On 24 May 1944 he accompanied three Marine pilots on a reconnaissance and strafing mission along the north-east coast of New Ireland, which was then occupied by the Japanese, looking for signs of Japanese activity.

> Out to the coast line — four [Vought F4U] Corsairs abreast, racing over the water — I am the closest one to land. The trees pass, a streak of green; the beach a band of yellow on my left. Is it a post a mile ahead in the water, or a man standing? It moves toward shore. It is a man.
>
> All Japanese or unfriendly natives on New Ireland — everything is a target — no restrictions — shoot whatever you see. I line up my sight. A mile takes ten seconds at our speed. At 1,000 yards my .50 calibers are deadly. I know just where they strike. I cannot miss.
>
> Now he is out of the water, but he does not run. The beach is wide. He cannot make the cover of the trees. He is centered in my sight. My finger tightens on the trigger. A touch, and he will crumple on the coral sand.

But he disdains to run. He strides across the beach. Each step carries dignity and courage in its timing. He is not an ordinary man. The shot is too easy. His bearing, his stride, his dignity — there is something in them that has formed a bond between us. His life is worth more than the pressure of a trigger. I do not want to see him crumple on the beach. I release the trigger.

I ease back on the stick. He reaches the tree line, merges with the streak of green on my left. I am glad I have not killed him. I would never have forgotten him writhing on the beach. I will always remember his figure striding over the sand, the fearless dignity of his steps. I had his life balanced on a muscle's twitch. I gave it back to him, and thank God that I did so. I shall never know who he was — Jap or native. But I realize that the life of this unknown stranger — probably an enemy — is worth a thousand times more to me than his death. I should never quite have forgiven myself if I had shot him — naked, courageous, defenceless, yet so unmistakably a man.[2]

Evidently, the man on the beach was utterly defenceless. But there are, of course, degrees of defencelessness. One could say, for example, that a novice pilot is practically helpless in combat with a great ace. But that would be stretching things too far. (Besides, in the event it would have no practical significance, for even supposing the ace were ready to spare any opponent who was completely helpless, he would have no way of verifying the fact.) For our purpose a reasonable definition of "helpless" would be: "Helpless to defend himself in any normal way", the word "normal" serving to exclude extreme acts like sacrificing one's own life by ramming the enemy plane.[3]

In the air war the clearest situation in which an airman is completely and unmistakably defenceless is when he has baled out and is descending in his parachute. This situation materialized for the first time in 1914. It was entirely new to warfare and there was a controversy whether it was against the rules of warfare to kill such a defenceless man. There was also an important distinction that somewhat complicated matters: was the parachuting man coming down within his own lines or in his enemy's territory? In the latter case the man would almost certainly become a prisoner-of-war and cease to be a threat to one's own side. To shoot at him would be an act of inhumanity. "One cannot say that there is any definite rule of war upon the point, but it may at least be affirmed that to attack a parachutist in circumstances in which he is certain in any case to be captured would be contrary to the principles of international law."[4] Moreover, apart from being a waste of ammunition, shooting the man would be a stupid thing to do, as you would kill a potential source of information.

When the man who had baled out came down over ground held by his side, however, he remained a combatant. This was nearly always the case in the First World War, because throughout the war both sides employed captive observation balloons equipped with parachutes and it was not until 1917 that parachutes were used to escape from disabled aeroplanes and then only by the Germans.[5] Now the observation balloons[6] (also called kite-balloons, "sausages" or — by the Germans — *Drachen* [kites]) were tethered to a winch on the ground, by means of which they were let up and hauled down again. So at all times they were over their own territory and if the observers in the basket underneath the balloon took to their parachutes when they were attacked by enemy planes, they invariably came down among their own people. Only when a balloon broke loose from its cable was it possible that the wind carried it over the enemy's lines before the crew managed to bale out.[7] Taking these circumstances into account, together with the fact that there is no record of a (necessarily German) airman being shot at after baling out of an aeroplane, it is easy to understand why, with few exceptions, men going down in parachutes in the *First* World War were men who would come down within their own lines. Consequently they remained combatants and would soon renew the fight. If you got the chance to kill them, would it not be foolish to spare them? As foolish as when in a hand-to-hand fight on the ground in which you had knocked your enemy's weapon out of his hand you then waited for him to pick it up and resume the fight?

Opinions (and actions) differed:

> My habit of attacking Huns dangling from parachutes led to many arguments in the mess. Some officers, of the Eton and Sandhurst type, thought it was "unsportsmanlike" to do it. Never having been to a public school, I was unhampered by

such considerations of "form". I just pointed out that there
was a bloody war on, and that I intended to avenge my pals.[8]

This is from a book by Ira ("Taffy") Jones, a fighter ace
in World War I, telling about his war experiences. The
book comprises (unedited) extracts from his 1918 diary. On
19 May 1918 he attacked a German observation balloon near
Armentières. In his diary he described it in these words:

> I had opened fire at about 200 yards' range, and kept at it
> until I got to within 40 yards. Two men jumped out of the
> balloon and to avoid colliding with it, I turned sharply to the
> right and then came back to it again. Then, for the first time
> in my life, I saw at close quarters a couple of men going down
> in parachutes. I immediately attacked them, one after the
> other. I could see no point in setting the cumbersome-
> looking "sausage" on fire if the observers were allowed to get
> away with their information and their lives. I think I hit
> them. I hope I did.[9]

Ten days later he recorded in his diary that the Germans had
shot down a couple of British balloons belonging to 25 and 39
Companies, in flames.

> I hear one observer was killed. When I write this, it goes
> against the grain. Killing an observer sounds unsporting, yet
> it is quite correct in principle. War is war. Really, a balloon
> observer must expect to be killed, like any other combatant.
> After all, he is responsible for many enemy casualties. I shall
> always try to kill the observer, if I can — distasteful as the
> job may be. "Kill or be killed" should be the airman's
> motto.[10]

Contemporary sources supply abundant evidence that attacks
on observers descending by parachute were recurrent events on
both sides.

Hauptmann Stottmeister, in a contribution to *Die deutschen
Luftstreitkräfte im Weltkriege* (1920; edited by G. P. Neuman),
says that the balloon observer's troubles were not over once he
had made his leap for safety with his parachute. "The attacking
aeroplane would direct a furious fire against the defenceless
man hanging from the parachute and blazing tracer bullets
would leap at him."[11] Allied observers received similar
treatment at the hands of German pilots. J. Mortane[12] gives

some examples of French observers being machine-gunned in their parachutes by German pilots.

An interesting case, related by Alan Morris in *The Balloonatics* (1970), was that of Lieutenant Thomas Kennie, the commanding officer of 37 Section. On 27 September 1917 he was alone in the basket of his balloon, observing enemy territory in the neighbourhood of Ablain St. Nazaire, when it was suddenly attacked by an Albatros fighter flown by Hans Waldhausen. Kennie jumped. The balloon was set on fire. From a nearby aerodrome Douglas Reed, a journalist then serving in an RE8 squadron, saw it fall "in a dissolving mass of crimson flame and smoke". He then saw that "the German turned on the little white speck beneath him that was the parachute of the balloon pilot. Machine-gunning hard he dived on the helpless swinging figure, rose-coloured in the sun's last rays. . . . Now, when he turned to go, two British chasers were on him. Three shining white machines, soaring, leaping, falling, charging, their tracer machine-gun bullets blazing a yellow trail, they rode about the darkening sky like silver knights jousting at each other with golden lances."[13] Waldhausen was hit by the British fighters. Wounded and with his engine stopped, he crash-landed. He could have made his escape if he had not lost valuable time in trying to kill Kennie. Ironically, Kennie came down unhurt.

The story has a sequel that is interesting because of a chivalrous act on the part of one of those involved. Waldhausen had been dragged out of his aeroplane by a group of Canadian soldiers who, incensed by the attack on Kennie, stripped him of his helmet and goggles, gloves, rank badges and wrist watch. No doubt worse would have followed, but for the arrival on the scene of 'Mick' Mannock, one of the British fighter pilots who had been out to get Waldhausen. He had landed about a mile from the wreck of the Albatros and run towards it. Mannock's hatred of Germans was a byword among his squadron mates. But now, armed with a Very pistol, he persuaded the Canadians to drop their threatening entrenching tools and to carry the bleeding German to a Casualty Clearing Station in a nearby cellar. His innate chivalry was a match for his hatred; he showed they could reside together in a man's breast.[14] Hans Waldhausen survived the war.

The machine-gunning of men dangling helplessly from their parachutes came to be accepted by many, if not always whole-heartedly. Indeed, one could even — as I have indicated earlier — put up a rational if rather cold-blooded defence of the practice, as an RAF captain did when he said in justification of the shooting of a balloonist by a German pilot:

> He was only doing his duty. . . . In wartime the soldier's task is to defeat the enemy, and to treat a falling balloon observer as though he were a non-combatant is a neglect of duty. He would not be a prisoner in all probability and as like as not he would be up in another balloon in a few days' time.
>
> Clearly, therefore, it was up to the German to put an end to him just as it was up to us to put an end to his opposite number. I have done it myself. I am not proud of the action but consider it fully justified.[15]

But, especially among the pilots themselves, the men who were expected and in some cases ordered to do the actual killing, disgust was often felt and expressed at shooting helpless men.

> The balloon itself was a legitimate target. But the moment an observer left his post his parachute should count as a white flag. To shoot him then would be cold-blooded murder. Thus the sentiment ran in all squadron messes; and if the balloon observers knew in their hearts that it was fallacious, naturally they did not argue.[16]

Captain A. C. Reid reports that

> It was always an unwritten code of honour amongst us not to fire on these unfortunate individuals in their disagreeable descent.[17]

Lieutenant Wellman, referring to two German observers floating down by parachutes from a balloon he was attacking, tells us that

> I might have killed them both in the air but I refrained, for they were unarmed, and the French and Americans do not make war on such.[18]

It could always happen, of course, that a pilot attacking a balloon unintentionally hit the observer who had just jumped from the basket. But bad aiming apart, and provided they did not use firearms, observers were safeguarded by such chivalry as existed in aerial combat.[19]

And — as we shall see later on — even if an observer used any firearm he was carrying, this did not necessarily mean he had then forfeited this safeguard.

To be sure, besides the moral restraint there was also a practical reason why pilots were reluctant to go at the observers. Attacking an observation balloon was a highly dangerous undertaking. They were heavily protected by anti-aircraft guns, which had one of the main problems of AA-gunners (the height the aircraft was flying at) solved before-hand, because they knew of course the exact height at which the balloon they protected was floating. The pilot attacking such a combative target would feel a strong natural urge to spend as little time as possible in the neighbourhood. Making another pass to make sure of the observers could easily prove self-defeating, as Hans Waldhausen found out to his cost.

Nevertheless, there were numerous instances in which such an attack was made. Sometimes retaliation was the motive.

> The attacking airman would sometimes fire a few rounds at the unfortunate observer who had jumped and was swinging and dangling from his parachute *en route* earthwards. The Germans were the first to indulge in this merciless practice; the RAF paid them back in their own coin. Watson*, for instance, in a balloon attack on 1st June [1918], with Cobby's patrol, shot through the rope of a descending observer's parachute.[20]

Returning evil for evil has been, through the centuries, an ever recurring source of brutalization of hostilities. It is mostly naïve to try to determine which side started a particular cruelty. So it is in this case.

Were pilots ever actually ordered to attack observers who had baled out? It seems that there were few explicit orders. J. N. Hall quotes a French operation order that in so many words ordered pilots to attack the observers in their parachutes after the balloon had been destroyed. It seemed to him "as near

---

* Capt. H. G. Watson, Australian Flying Corps.

the borderline between legitimate warfare and cold-blooded murder as anything could well be".[21] And Lieutenant-Colonel Rougevin-Baville, later Director of France's *Musée de l'Air*, declared that "It would be silly to pretend that there were no orders to attack not only the balloons but their occupants."[22] Direct orders were mostly shunned; "strong advice" was given instead:

> At the Battle of Arras some RFC Wings passed the word that parachutists should not be spared, but little response was discernible.
>
> On May 28 [1917] General Allenby, Third Army commander, called to congratulate 40 Squadron on its anti-balloon stunts and strongly advised the assembly to shoot balloon occupants in future. Direct orders were waived, and indeed they would have been unenforceable. Tracer could always "miss". The fighting generally would become more squalid before the handful of pilots convinced themselves that such mean killings were necessary.[23]

The last sentence of this quotation might prompt the question whether there were, towards the end of the war, any pilots left who refused to shoot at parachuting men. The answer is yes, there certainly were. One of them was Frank Luke, an American from Arizona, one of the wildest and most spectacular air fighters of all time. He had only been in action for two months when he was killed on 26 September 1918, but in that short time he became America's leading ace.[24] He came to be called the Balloon Buster when he made destroying balloons his speciality; 14 of his 18 confirmed victories were observation balloons. On 14 September 1918 he was ordered to attack a troublesome kite-ballloon at Buzy. With his friend Joe Wehner guarding his tail, he went at the balloon and brought it down in flames. Then eight Fokkers dived on him. Luke's SPAD received several hits and he could not fight back because his guns jammed. But Wehner (who, four days later, was to give his life in defending Luke) made a furious attack on the Fokkers and they both got away from them. Luke managed to get his machine-guns going again and shortly afterwards attacked another enemy balloon, near Boigneville. Six times he dived at it. During his first attack the observer, *Vizefeldwebel* Muenchhoff, shot at him with a Parabellum light machine-gun, while his companion, *Signalauswerter* Gasser, jumped out of the basket. Then he, too, baled out. Both floated slowly earthward, offering excellent targets for Luke's guns, but, in spite of the fact that he had been shot at, he made no attempt to fire upon them. "Why didn't you get that observer?" Luke was asked. "Hell," he replied, "the poor devil was helpless!"[25] And that coming from a man who has been described as one who "used the tactics and brutality of the dock walloper, the knee-in-the-gut attack of the bar brawler, the everything-goes code of the gutter bully. Had he ever encountered a captured airman he in all probability would have dismembered him with his bare hands."[26] This, especially the last sentence, does not sound very convincing in view of his behaviour towards Muenchhoff and Gasser.

After our survey of a number of representative cases in which pilots in the First World War either shot at, or refrained from shooting at men going down in parachutes over their own ground, we may sum up the matter as follows: (1) International law did not cover the matter. (2) There were not any other official rules to go by. (3) No usage had developed in the matter yet. (4) As a result, on each particular occasion the issue was more or less decided by the pilot's sense of duty and/ or by (usually strong) personal feelings, either of hatred and revenge, or of a gentlemanly, chivalrous nature.

So much for the First World War.

Between the two great wars a serious effort was made to formulate international rules concerning air warfare. In the winter of 1922-23 a Commission of jurists from six countries — the United States, Britain, France, Italy, the Netherlands and Japan — met at The Hague to prepare a draft code for the consideration of their governments. These Rules of Air Warfare 1923 remained a draft, however, chiefly because the French government considered a special body of laws for the air to be unnecessary. The code was never embodied in an international Convention and therefore had no binding force. Nevertheless, the Rules have had some influence upon the practice of belligerent and neutral governments.[27] The proposed code included the following article:

> Article 20: When an aircraft has been disabled, the occupants, when endeavouring to escape by means of a parachute, must not be attacked in the course of their descent.

The learned gentlemen must have had their reasons for not making the important distinction between airmen going down on friendly soil and those landing in hostile territory. It is unlikely that they should have overlooked the point: it is a fundamental one and had already been brought forward in the 1914-1918 war. Probably they were indeed of the opinion that all airmen descending by parachute must be immune from attack, regardless which side held the territory they landed in. But then one would have expected them to include that clause in article 20, to make it unambiguous.

Anyway, as the Rules were never legalized, the question whether it is wrong (in all, or only in certain, circumstances) to try to kill somebody who is descending by parachute after having jumped out of a disabled aircraft has remained a moral issue. How each individual man handled this problem, why he decided one way or the other, depended on many things, sometimes even on his mood of the moment, but to a large extent on the system of ethics he called his own and felt associated with. And it is here that chivalry had a chance to come into play.

Before turning to the Second World War, it is necessary to pay some attention to the minor wars that preceded it in the 'thirties. In 1935 the Italians invaded and conquered Ethiopia. Although their air force played a not unimportant part in the military operations, it did not meet any air opposition, so from our present point of view this war need not concern us.

The Manchurian incident in 1931, followed by a number of others in all of which aircraft took part, led to the outbreak in 1937 of the Sino-Japanese War. There is little material available on the period of that war before December 1941, when it became part of the Second World War. Even less is on hand concerning the short and largely unnoted Russo-Japanese conflicts in 1938 (on the Soviet-Korean border) and 1939 (on the border of Mongolia and Manchuria). These Far-Eastern conflicts played an important part in the development of air warfare. But they have not yielded any data that could be used in the context of our present book, except for the incident I have already related in chapter 2, as an illustration of the vast difference there was between Western and Eastern ethics of warfare.

46

The Second World War had a prelude in Europe, too. In the summer of 1936 General Franco took up arms against the Spanish Republican (Communist) government and started a civil war that was to last nearly three years. Before long three foreign powers stepped in, Italy and Germany on the side of the Nationalists (Fascists), Russia on the Communist side. To them Spain was an ideal testing ground for trying out their new weapons and tactics. So the Spanish Civil War became a major conflict, in which important lessons were learned, especially in the air war, though they were not always assimilated or even fully understood by those in power.

What about chivalrous behaviour? Was there any evidence of that? One would not expect much, civil wars being notorious for their savagery. Still, remarkably few instances can be found in which pilots fighting one another in the Spanish skies stooped to inhuman acts, whereas chivalry was not absent. Barring the bombing of towns, in which there can never be a place for honour, it appears that the war in the air distinguished itself favourably from that on the ground, as was the case in the First World War. There were some nasty incidents all the same. On 4 June 1938 a pilot of the Italian *Gamba de Ferro* group had to bale out of his Fiat CR 32 fighter over Linares de Mora. Floating down in his parachute he was machine-gunned to death.[28] It is not clear on which side of the lines he was coming down.

In a book written by a Spanish fighter pilot on the Republican side, Francisco Tarazona Torán, we find the following passage:

> 22 September 1938. This morning, when I talked with my pilots, I was told that the pilot of the Sixth who had baled out had been machine-gunned while he was hanging from his parachute. They did the same to Ruiz[29] over Nules. Just what difference do those buffoons make between shooting at a damaged aircraft and killing a pilot who has baled out? I do not know. One must have the stomach for it, perhaps it also depends on your education. I do not believe that the Spanish fascists have done it. They differ from us in ideology, it is true, but they are Spaniards.[30]

In the last sentence but one there is, of course, stress on the word 'Spanish'. Tarazona wants to distinguish his compatriots from the Italians and Germans who fought alongside the Nationalists. It is impossible to say to what extent his trust in the Nationalist Spaniards was warranted. In at least one case it was clearly fully justified. On 2 September 1938 the Nationalist fighter ace Ángel Salas Larrazábal, commander of the *Gruppo* 2-G-3, destroyed three Tupolev SB-2 bombers in quick succession over the Badajoz area. He then turned on one of the Polikarpov I-16 (Mosca) fighters that were escorting the bombers and shot it down, too. The pilot, José Redondo Martín (CO of the *1a Escuadrilla de Moscas*, and, by the way, son of the mayor of Madrid), baled out. Salas followed his defeated enemy down, flying protective cover round the man in the parachute, who came down in his territory. Salas then waved to him and flew off. Redondo waved back.[31] This incident received a lot of publicity on the Republican side, and after the war General Franco mentioned it in his foreword to the book *Guerra en el Aire* (Madrid 1940) by Joaquín García Morato, who with 40 victories was the most successful Spanish fighter pilot. Franco compared Salas's chivalrous behaviour with the knightly courtesy of medieval times.

The very fact that Salas thought it necessary to protect a helpless enemy from other Nationalist pilots is evidence that it was not unusual to attack such a man. And there is not any reason to suppose that the other side behaved differently. But it is the fine exceptions that count in our search for chivalrous behaviour in the air wars.

When the Spanish Civil War ended in March 1939 the Second World War was about to begin. In this war tens of thousands of aircrew saved their lives by parachute. They — and all the airmen in the wars between 1918 and 1939 who rescued themselves by baling out — jumped from aeroplanes; observation balloons were never used again after the First World War. Nor were airships in a combat role, but the crews of the Zeppelins the Germans used in World War I had no parachutes.

The Second World War saw the first use in actual war of troops dropped by parachute behind the enemy lines, with their arms and equipment.[32] There could not be any doubt that it was lawful to shoot at these paratroops (as they came to be called) while they were still in the air. There were, however, some confusing situations in which defenders did not know or claimed they could not know that, for example, the ten-man crew of a bomber coming down in parachutes was not a small body of paratroopers.

In the Second World War there was still no definite answer to the question whether parachuting aircrew in distress must or need not be immune from attack. Still, the situation differed from that in the First World War, if only slightly. The point had at least been under discussion and, although the resulting rule (article 20) was not law, it could give some support to any authority that wished to include this or a similar rule in particular orders, instructions or manuals. In fact, it seems to have been done on both the British and the German side. The German fighter pilots had standing orders never to shoot at airmen going down in parachutes.[33] As for the British side, now and again one finds a reference to "the rules".

On the morning of 30 August 1940 (during the Battle of Britain) Pilot Officer D. N. O. Jenkins (253 Sqn) had to bale out of his Hawker Hurricane (P3921) after combat with enemy fighters over Redhill. While coming down by parachute he was shot dead by the pilot of a Messerschmitt Bf 109. Peter Townsend, in his book *Duel of Eagles* (1970), wrote in connection with this occurrence: "By the rules of war it was justifiable to kill a pilot who could fight again. But few of us could bring ourselves to shoot a helpless man in cold blood."[34]

On 23 September 1940 Squadron Leader J. A. Kent (303 Polish Sqn) shot down a Messerschmitt Bf 109 over the Channel. The German pilot baled out. Kent describes what happened then:

> The 109 dived straight into the sea, while he, apparently unhurt, drifted down in his parachute. I circled round him a couple of times and felt it might be kinder to shoot him as he had one hell of a long swim, but I could not bring myself to do it.
>
> Without waiting for him to hit the water I turned for home. [. . .] The Poles were fed up with me when I admitted that I could not bring myself to shoot the chap in the parachute and they reminded me of events earlier in the month when we were told that one or two pilots of No.1 Squadron had baled out and had then been shot by German fighters. At the time the Poles had asked me if it was true that this was happening.

49

I had to tell them that, as far as I knew, it was, at which they asked: 'Oh, can we?' I explained that, distasteful as it was, the Germans were within their rights in shooting our pilots over this country and that, if one of us shot down a German aircraft over France and the pilot baled out, then we were quite entitled to shoot him. But this was not so over England as, aside from anything else, he would be out of the war and might even be a very useful source of information for us. They thought about this for a bit and then said: 'Yes, we understand — but what if he is over the Channel?' — to which I jokingly replied: 'Well, you can't let the poor bugger drown, can you?' This remark was quite seriously thrown in my teeth when they heard about the 109 pilot I had just shot down. There was no doubt about it, the Poles were playing the game for keeps far more than we were.[35]

It is not clear what rules Squadron Leaders Townsend and Kent refer to, but it should be noted that they both point out that it makes all the difference whether the parachuting man comes down on friendly or on hostile territory, the distinction that — as we have seen — article 20 of the Rules of Air Warfare 1923 surprisingly did not make.

The following is a passage from the post-battle report of Air Chief Marshal Sir Hugh Dowding, Commander-in-Chief of Fighter Command during the Battle of Britain:

This is perhaps a convenient opportunity to say a word about the ethics of shooting at aircraft crews who have baled out in parachutes. Germans descending over England are prospective prisoners-of-war and, as such, should be immune. On the other hand, British pilots descending over England are still potential combatants. Much indignation was caused by the fact that German pilots sometimes fired on our descending airmen (although, in my opinion, they were perfectly entitled to do so), but I am glad to say that in many cases they refrained.[36]

Dowding's use of the words "ethics" (where "law" could not be used) and "in my opinion" indicate the lack of any hard-and-fast rule and the vagueness that prevailed in this matter.

Incidentally, if one realizes that Dowding wrote this in 1941, reporting on a fierce battle he had just fought under agonizing stress, and at a time when his country was still in a most desperate situation, one is struck by the restraint and fairness with which he speaks of his enemies. True, the battle had been won, and Dowding had occasion to be magnanimous. However that may be, his words are impressive and reminiscent of one of the primary virtues of the ideal knight: courtesy, also towards one's enemy.

Indeed, both sides in the Battle of Britain deserve praise for the fairness they generally displayed in those nearly four months of hard, and at times bitter, fighting. For, however stringent their respective rules may have been by which they were supposed to fight, these alone could not control the actions of the pilots, whose emotions were raised to such a high pitch in combat that they were apt to act impulsively. The rules must have been backed up by an ingrained sense of fairness.

What happened to Flight-Lieutenant J. W. C. Simpson (43 Sqn) on 19 July 1940 is a fair example of chivalrous behaviour on the German side. On that day he was shot down off Selsey Bill during a combat with Messerschmitt Bf 109s of *III/JG27*, probably by *Oberleutnant* Walter Adolph. After Simpson had baled out

> one of the Me.109s began circling him. 'I was alarmed. He was near enough for me to see his face. I felt . . . he would shoot me . . . but he behaved well. The noise of his aircraft was terrific. He flew round me . . . then he suddenly . . . waved to me.' And the chivalrous German fighter pilot then dived for home.[37]

Less noble behaviour occurred, too, as was to be expected. But ruthless acts were few. I have not found a single case in which a German pilot descending by parachute over Britain was machine-gunned. And not many pilots in the Battle of Britain died in the cruel way P/O Jenkins did: going down in a parachute, relieved and happy in the belief that he had escaped death, and then seeing an enemy fighter deliberately turn on him, with the sickening realization that he was going to be killed after all.

Also, in some cases there is room for genuine doubt whether the killing was indeed intentional or even whether enemy fire was in fact the cause that a pilot who had baled out was dead when he reached the ground. Aerial combat involving many aircraft is a most confusing, sometimes even chaotic event and it is easy to be mistaken in one's observations. In the afternoon

51

of 15 September 1940 Sergeant L. Pidd (238 Sqn), during a combat over Kenley with Heinkel He 111s and Messerschmitt Bf 110s, baled out of his Hawker Hurricane fighter. He landed dead, however. Sergeant S.E. Bann from the same squadron saw it happen and the following day he wrote in a letter to his parents:

> We're all just mad for revenge. Never again shall any one of us give any mercy for our poor Flight Commander and yesterday the Yorkshire boy Sgt. Pidd fell victims to these swines, machine-gunning whilst [they were] coming down by parachute. Now, after seeing poor Pidd go, shall I ever forgive the 'Hun'?[38]

In the Brenzett Aeronautical Museum, which excavated the wreck of Sergeant Pidd's Hurricane (P2836) in 1975, some parts of the aircraft are on display. The accompanying text reads, in part: "Sgt. L. Pidd baled out but was killed when his parachute failed to open." No mention is made of the enemy firing on him after he had baled out (which, to be sure, could be the cause of the parachute failure).*

One of the many who have testified that the war between the British and German air forces was fought with great fairness, was the famous German fighter pilot Adolf Galland, who wrote:

> It is with deep satisfaction that I can state that, however hard the fighting was, it never for a moment deviated from the unwritten laws of chivalry. Far from being humanitarian dreamers, and fully conscious of the fact that our conflict with the enemy was a struggle that could only end in either of two ways, victory or death, we observed the rules of fair fighting, the first one of which is to spare a helpless enemy. [. . .] to shoot at a pilot hanging in a parachute would have seemed to us at the time an act of unthinkable barbarity.[39]

In this context Galland reports on an interesting conversation he had with *Reichsmarschall* Hermann Göring during the Battle of Britain. In the course of this conversation, at which Werner Mölders, *Kommodore* of *JG51*, and a great friend of Galland's, was the only other person present, Göring remarked

* In the afternoon of 28 September 1940 Sergeant S. E. Bann baled out over Brading Marshes, after his Hurricane had been severely damaged during combat with Bf 109s. His parachute failed to open.

Ernst Udet (left) during a visit to fighter units along the northern coast of France, chatting with Adolf Galland (middle) and Werner Mölders (right), Germany's leading aces then, on 4 September 1940.

(Bundesarchiv)

on the fact that in the case of highly developed weapons like aircraft the crew was worth far more than the machine. It was much easier to replace the aircraft than the man who could fly it. A well-trained and experienced pilot was worth his weight in gold. All this led up to a question: "What would you think of an order to kill pilots who have baled out during a combat over England?" He looked Galland in the eyes. "I should regard that as murder, *Herr Reichsmarschall*," Galland answered, "and try all possible means to resist such an order." Göring then laid his hands on Galland's shoulders and said: "It was exactly the answer I had expected from you, Galland." Galland states he does not know the background to Göring's sounding him out on the subject, but he leaves us in no doubt that he considers it impossible that the idea originated with Göring himself.[40]

So here again, as we did when we dealt with the First World War, we learn of an attempt by someone in high office to effect orders to shoot at parachuting airmen. This particular attempt met with similar resistance from those who would have had to

53

carry them out. But, regrettably, there is no denying that in the
Second World War such instructions were in force in the
British, American and German air forces, though it is
practically certain that they were not operative in all units and
at all times. My efforts to get at the complete truth concerning
orders like that have not been successful. There has been a
general reticence to publish, discuss or even mention them.
This, as a matter of fact, is indicative of a distinct feeling of
shame about such instructions, even though they were not
unlawful. That feeling, in turn, would prove that those
concerned were not left unperturbed by the ethics of the
matter.

Let me present some evidence of the existence of the
discreditable orders.

On the night of 18 June 1940 a Bristol Blenheim of 604 Sqn
shot down a "large twin-engined seaplane" off the French coast
between Griz Nez and Calais . . .

> the German seaplane crashed into the sea and the lights went
> out. Tommy went on firing as the Blenheim passed low over
> the crashed aircraft, for which he was later reproached on the
> grounds of cruelty. That was, of course, utter nonsense. As
> he pointed out himself, it was clearly laid down how the
> gunners were to deal with enemy aircrew over their own
> territory and what procedure was to be followed. He was
> doing no more than obeying instructions.[41]

Although this is not a case of parachuting airmen, the principle
is the same: they were completely helpless.

There is no doubt that

> Most American pilots refused to fire upon downed enemy
> fighter pilots. However, some American commanders ordered
> the pilots to strafe downed enemy jet pilots so they could not
> return to fight again.[42]

The pilots of the jet fighters, mostly Messerschmitt Me 262s,
were, of course, singled out because they were known or could
be assumed to be Germany's surviving experienced fighter
pilots, flying the only type of aircraft that could still become a
serious menace to the air superiority which the USAAF had
gained in the daylight skies over Germany.

Adolf Galland writes that when during his last sortie of the war, on 26 April 1945, his Me 262 was seriously damaged in combat, he was terrified at the prospect of having to bale out and then be shot while coming down by parachute. "We jet-fighter pilots knew from experience that we had to reckon with that."[43]

Orders or no, it is a fact that on numerous occasions US fighters killed or tried to kill Me 262 pilots after they had baled out, and not only Me 262 pilots. One finds accounts of such attacks in several sources[44], occasionally in an official report. On 1 November 1944 *Oberfeldwebel* Willi Banzaff, after shooting down a North American P-51 fighter, tried to attack a group of Boeing B-17 bombers returning from a raid on Gelsenkirchen and Rüdesheim. But his Me 262 was intercepted by American fighters from three Fighter Groups, the 20th, 56th and 352nd FG.

> Then, in the terse wording of the 56th FG report: 'After repeated hits jet started to smoke; pilot jettisoned canopy and baled out, 8,000 ft. Two unidentified P-51s in vicinity shot at pilot on chute.' Credit for shooting down the Me 262 was shared between [Lieutenant Walter] Groce [56th FG] and Lieutenant William Gerbe of the 352nd FG. In spite of the unchivalrous conduct of two of his foes, Banzaff reached the ground safely.[45]

Apart from the threat emanating from the appearance, in July 1944, of the Me 262 jet fighter,[46] was there any other reason that about this time the Americans started attacking German pilots descending by parachute in increasing numbers? Major Walther Dahl, *Kommodore* of *JG300*, thought there was. On 15 September 1944 he told *Reichsmarschall* Hermann Göring that for the last two months there had been more and more reports of German pilots being shot at while descending by parachute. He then expressed his opinion that this was partly due to Himmler's deplorable directive to the higher police officials in Germany, in which he had stated that it was not the task of the police to intervene in altercations between Germans and Allied airmen who had landed by parachute. There had been lynchings of unfortunate airmen who had fallen into the hands of a population embittered by the indiscriminate bombing of their homes. Dahl contended that Himmler's indirect order to the police not to stop such lynchings had provoked the Americans to retaliate against German airmen who had baled out. According to Dahl, Göring agreed with him and promised to do his best to have the directive revoked. Dahl goes on to say:

> In an order he issued to the Luftwaffe, Göring quite decidedly spoke out against tolerating the lynching of *Terrorflieger*, and it is in keeping with his correct and chivalrous attitude that in his opinion pilots who had committed a crime against military law should be court-martialled.[47]

That shooting at helpless men in parachutes occurred rather more often than is compatible with fair combat, should not blind us to the fact that the great majority of the pilots, Allied or German, wanted no part in such killings. It is not unlikely that some of them were even unaware that it was done by their countrymen at all. The following passage from a book by an American fighter pilot certainly gives that impression:

> A few seconds later I saw ahead of me the parachuting pilot of the 109 I had shot (scared) down a few minutes before. Pointing the plane at him, I flipped the gun switch to "camera only" to get a picture, but the thought crossed my mind that this circuit had been known to foul up and fire the guns, so, I restrained my desire to get a confirming picture of my victim. Instead I turned aside, passing within thirty feet of him. I suppose when he saw me point straight at him, he fully expected to be gunned down, for he had drawn himself up and crossed his arms in front of his face as if to ward off the bullets, and when he saw me turn aside without firing, and waggling my wings as I passed he started waving his arms and grinning like a Cheshire cat. I thought as I climbed that since he had provided me with my tenth victory, he deserved a break. I just hoped he'd live to spread the word that Americans didn't shoot helpless pilots in parachutes. Maybe the Germans would follow suit.[48]

This happened on 16 March 1944 over Germany. A few months later, on 28 June, the same pilot (Captain Richard E. Turner, commanding officer of the 356th Fighter Squadron, 354th FG) shot down a Messerschmitt 109 over Caen (Normandy). In his words:

> Half a second later the tumbling body of the pilot dropped

from the clouds, where it was jerked up short in its fall by the opening chute. As I circled the chute the German clasped his hands over his head, and shook them as if to tell me he was OK. [. . .] I dispatched the rest of my flight back to patrol duty, but I stayed to circle the German pilot in his descent to earth, where I figured he would probably be captured by the English troops around Caen. There were still a lot of Spitfires buzzing around, and I had heard that some of the British pilots who had survived the Battle of Britain were inclined to be pretty bitter about allowing German pilots safe descent after bail out. Personally, I gave little credence to this rumor, but since I was responsible for the poor devil's being in this predicament, I decided it was the least I could do to give him a fighting chance to survive, as he was no longer a threat to the invasion operations. Besides, he quite possibly might have valuable information for the interrogation people. At any rate, I knew if our positions were reversed, I would appreciate similar treatment from a German. So I continued to fly around the pilot as he floated down to the outskirts of Caen, where I could see English troops rushing to the probable landing area.[49]

The best of intentions to fight fair, even an innate sense of chivalry, could sometimes be suddenly invalidated (mostly temporarily) by feelings of hatred and revenge, caused by seeing or hearing of a cruelty committed by the enemy. P. B. ('Laddie') Lucas describes a case like that in his introduction to a book on the air battle for Malta (where he served for a few months in 1942, with 249 Sqn.).

Much has been made of the gunning of pilots, as they floated to safety in their parachutes; but it was the exception to prove the rule of hard, clean, ruthless fighting in the air. I personally saw it happen but once — to a fine Rhodesian pilot in 249 named Douggie Leggo. Bounced out of the sun by the German ace, Neuhoff, whom 249 then shot down, Leggo rolled his Spitfire onto its back and parted company. His parachute opened immediately. As he descended earthwards, a lone Messerschmitt, appearing seemingly from nowhere, sprayed the canopy with tracer bullets in a callous gesture of murder. It was over in seconds. There was no chance of retaliation.

No discipline will hold the blind fury of a squadron which has witnessed such cruelty to a comrade. I knew it could only be a question of days before one of the pilots, surreptitiously would find a chance of levelling the score. It came within a week. A Junkers 88 had been shot down south-west of the island. The aircraft had ditched in the sea and now the crew of three were in a dinghy ten miles or so from Delimara Point. Their chances of being picked up must have been good. The sea was calm and sparkling. A Dornier 24 would have had no trouble making a landing. As we headed home for Takali, my eye caught sight of a single Spitfire away to my left, at the bottom of a shallow, fast dive, heading straight for the dinghy. A sustained burst of fire sent geysers of sea water creeping up on the tiny, inflated boat. Not content with one run, the pilot pulled up into a tight climbing turn to the left and dived again. In war, one bad act will always beget another. . . .[50]

The point is also illustrated by what a Lancaster bomber pilot writes about an ugly scene he witnessed during a raid on Berlin, his reaction to it, and a conversation he had about it afterwards:

I had no strong views about the pilots of night-fighters who opposed us in the campaign over Germany, and certainly no antipathy, until the night I saw a bomber crew bale out over the western suburbs of Berlin, and the pilot of an Me 109 fired burst after burst of gunfire at the figures swinging helplessly below their parachutes. First I felt sickened at the scene, silhouetted against the fires and smoke below, then I grew hot with anger at the bloody, vengeful act. I mentioned the incident later in the flight office, and said that now I took a harsher view of German pilots.

'I'm finished with all that balls about the Jerry pilots being just like us. I couldn't have shot those parachutes up.'

The Gunnery Leader shrugged, and commented:

'He may have been a Berliner himself, and he might have lost a wife, or his favourite popsy, in a raid last week. You never know.'

'Okay, and so have some of our chaps lost relatives in the blitz, but it hasn't turned them into murderous bastards, like that fellow.'

'How do you know it hasn't? It's a murderous bloody war, old mate.'[51]

Even a rumour about a parachute killing could be enough to rouse the pilots to vindictive anger. Reporting on the air war over Tunisia in 1942-3, which by all accounts was fought extremely fairly (as was all aerial combat in North Africa), Flight-Lieutenant D. I. Benham (242 Sqn.) writes:

> In the main it was the fairest campaign I ever knew; on one occasion a rumour went round that one of the pilots at Souk el Khemis had been shot while parachuting, and we were all very upset. For about 24 hours after hearing that we would probably have fired on a German pilot in the same predicament, but generally the fighting was very fair and we had a high regard for the enemy.[52]

It was not always a craving for revenge, motivated by some brutality perpetrated by the enemy, which made a man act viciously. Under the extreme strain of combat something else, a sudden shock of fear for instance, could trigger a senseless, savage act, which could not possibly be construed as one of retaliation. Wing-Commander J. R. D. ('Bob') Braham, CO of 141 Sqn, tells us about such an irrational reaction of himself. On the night of 17/18 August 1943, flying a Bristol Beaufighter equipped with radar, operated by his navigator, Flight-Lieutenant L. H. Jacobs, he shot down two Messerschmitt Bf 110s. The second victory, near Ameland, was a spectacular affair:

> There was a blinding flash as the Me exploded in my face. Our Beau rocked violently, threatening to flick over on its back. My windscreen was flecked with oil from the exploding wreckage which hurtled seawards. "God, that was close," was all I could say. Then as we circled I saw in the light of the moon a parachute floating gently downwards. Something made my blood boil. Perhaps it was the narrow escape from the collision that angered me, or maybe it was because I was exhausted. I called Jacko on the intercom. "One of the bastards must have been blown clear, I'm going to finish him off." I had turned towards the parachute when Jacko said, "Bob, let the poor blighter alone." This brought me to my senses and I felt ashamed at what I had intended to do. As we flew past the forlorn figure dangling on the end of the 'chute and falling towards the sea I wished I could call out to him that his life had been spared because of the compassion of my AI operator — a Jew like many of those the Nazis had slaughtered in the ghettoes and concentration camps of Europe.[53]

In the Pacific theatre of war the atmosphere was so strongly affected by feelings of hate and revenge that it is no wonder that chivalrous behaviour was rare and inhumanity common, on both sides. Pilots descending in parachutes were regularly shot at. But even so, there were exceptions. When Charles Lindbergh visited the 475th Fighter Group (known as "Satan's Angels") of the Fifth Air Force, based at Hollandia (Dutch New Guinea) on 26 June 1944,

> the talk drifted to air combats and parachute jumps. All of the pilots insisted it was proper to shoot enemy airmen coming down in their parachutes. However, several said that they themselves would not do it. "The Japs started it. If they want to play that way, we can, too." Accounts were given of American airmen shot down hanging from their parachutes by the Japanese.[54]

A much publicized story tells of a Japanese who, when his machine-gun fire failed to hit a parachuting American, resorted to a most unusual method. It happened during a big dogfight near the Russell Islands, on 7 June 1943.

> Twenty-two-year-old Lieut. Samuel S. Logan of VMF-112 [flying a Vought F4U Corsair] was hit as he went to the rescue of a New Zealand P-40 and baled out of his burning plane at 20,000 feet, whereupon a Japanese fighter pilot began making repeated runs on him. He was unsuccessful in shooting Logan so he finally tried to cut him up with his propeller. He did succeed in chopping off part of Logan's right foot and left heel but Flight Leader Herrich of the RNZAF drove off the would-be butcher. The marine completed his descent and was rescued at sea by a Grumman Duck piloted by Lieut.-Colonel Nathanial S. Clifford of MAG-21.[55]

It is unlikely that in the air war which the Germans fought against the Russians, from 1941 to 1945, the atmosphere was any better than in the Pacific. Nevertheless, in the available (German) literature on that theatre of war there are no references to killings of men going down in parachutes. In view of the none-too-gentlemanly way the Soviet Russians waged war, this is surprising. An explanation may be that they had sense — and restraint — enough to let Germans who had baled out come down unharmed, so that, after they had been pumped for information and (if they were famous aces) paraded in front of the press, they could be used as forced labourers.[56] The nature of the air war over Russia was such that the great majority of the Germans baling out came down in Russian-held territory or fell into the hands of partisans operating behind the German lines. So they were lost to the Luftwaffe anyway.

I have given a good deal of attention to the issue of shooting or not shooting at airmen descending by parachute, because a refusal to kill one's enemy in this particular situation, even though it is not unlawful, is the plainest representation to be found in the air wars of sparing a helpless enemy's life. But there were, of course, other situations in which a pilot did not wish to degrade himself by killing a defenceless adversary, although he had the right to do so, and — it could be argued — it was also his duty. The word "degrade" points the way to a most interesting element that can play a part in a man's generosity towards his defenceless adversary, especially if the enemy's plight is the direct result of the victor's prowess in arms. It is the element of arrogance. In sparing his enemy's life he may intimate, consciously or subconsciously, that he can afford to do that, as he has proved himself to be the stronger, to be a warrior of a higher grade. This point is well illustrated by what happened to the French ace Charles Nungesser on 12 September 1917. On that day,

> taking off from Dunkerque to fly to Paris for a rest, he was set upon by a Halberstadt. A dogfight ensued with the two contestants so well matched that neither was able to get in a burst at the other. Eventually, Nungesser, recognising that he had met his match, decided to land at Le Touquet aerodrome, apprehensive for the burst from behind that he felt would come. But the Halberstadt followed him in, landed some 30 yards away, taxied alongside, whereupon the pilot waved in salute — and took off again! Nungesser himself then took off again, and tried to find his chivalrous opponent, but was unable to do so. Nevertheless, *he felt humiliated*, and on arriving at Issy, asked the Nieuport company for an aeroplane that would let him wipe out this *blot on his honour!*[57] [author's italics.]

Few pilots can have been so determined to fight absolutely fair as Eddie Rickenbacker who, on 10 March 1918, wrote in his flight diary:

> Resolved today that hereafter I will never shoot at a Hun who is at a disadvantage, regardless of what he would do if he were in my position.

In truth, a remarkable and extreme point of view. Later he wrote about this:

> Just what influenced me to adopt that principle and even to enter it into my diary I have forgotten. That was very early in my fighting days and I had then had but few combats in the air. But with American fliers the war has always been more or less a sporting proposition and the desire for fair play prevents a sportsman from looking at the matter in any other light, even though it be a case of life or death. However that may be, I do not recall a single violation of this principle by any American aviator that I should care to call my friend.[58]

The last eight words form an intriguing restrictive clause, which Rickenbacker does not clarify.

Inevitably, it occasionally happened that someone killed a defenceless man without being aware of the fact that his victim had no means of defending himself. If the realization came to him afterwards, this could produce in him feelings of embarrassment or even distress.

One day in late July 1917 five pilots of 40 Sqn RFC, Flight Commander Lloyd (called "Zulu" because he was a South African), Tudhope, Kennedy, Mannock (not yet famous then) and MacLanachan, were flying a patrol near Valenciennes, when they spied five aeroplanes far below them. They dived towards them. The machines were German two-seaters, flying a complete rectangle in perfect formation. The RFC pilots each singled out their counterpart in the German flight and attacked, preparing themselves to face the defensive fire of the observers in the rear seats. MacLanachan thought it strange that the observer of the plane he attacked allowed him to reach point-blank range without showing any signs of defending himself. He opened fire and the German machine dived away, obviously out of control.

> Only then the truth dawned on me. The observer had been clear in my sight, he had been looking at me, but he had made no attempt to fire, *because he had no gun*. The flight had evidently been practising formation flying and, being low down so far from the front, had never thought of the possibility of attack.

The American ace Captain Eddie Rickenbacker beside his SPAD XIII. Note the "Hat-in-the-Ring" insignia of the 94th Aero Squadron.

(Smithsonian Institute)

Landing back at their base, the four other pilots, especially Mick Mannock, were enthusiastic about the five victories the flight had won, until MacLanachan told them he was convinced they had shot down a group of pupils in unarmed planes. Had any of the others been fired at? No, they had to acknowledge, they had not. Lloyd had been smiling, but now his face wrinkled into a frown.

> 'That explains it then. I thought there was something tame about the whole thing,' Zulu said, and after a few seconds, 'But look here then, we can't damn well hand in combat reports.'
> Zulu was always prepared to do the chivalrous act in his own unassuming way.
> 'It was pure cold-blooded murder,' I said, laughing at the shock to the others' sporting instincts.
> Zulu laughed too. 'And to think that we've shot down five poor innocents.'
> We agreed that under the circumstances we would not send in any claims nor expect any kudos for our empty victory. We did not tell the others.[59]

A true fighter does not find satisfaction in a victory that is too easily won, not even when his adversary does have the means to defend himself but does not properly do so. Just as a hunter experiences no thrill when the shot is too easy.[60]

On 12 May 1940 Adolf Galland and his wingman, flying at 11,000 feet over Belgium, near Liège, saw eight Hawker Hurricanes below them. They dived on the British fighters, whose pilots were oblivious to the imminent danger. "Come on, defend yourself," Galland thought when he lined up one of the Hurricanes in his sights and drew nearer and nearer. "You really ought to give him a warning," he said to himself when the pilot still showed no sign of being aware of the enemy behind him. Hits from Galland's first burst shocked the Hurricane pilot into a rather clumsy evasive manoeuvre, which brought him into the line of fire of the other German. One more attack and it was all over: the Hurricane went down out of control and crashed. The seven other Hurricanes fled in all directions, but Galland shot one of them down, too. They were his first victories, but

I had not experienced any thrill and was not even exactly

happy with my success. Such feelings did not come until much later, when we came to grips with stronger adversaries, when each combat inexorably decided the question 'You or I?' But this day I nearly had something like a bad conscience. And the congratulations from my superiors and comrades did not taste quite right.[61]

From killing a defenceless enemy who is aware of your presence it is only a step to killing an enemy who does not even know you are there, ready to attack him. But to the mind of the fair-fighting man it is an essential step, which crosses the borderline between the sphere of improper and that of proper fighting. Why exactly? Because the circumstance that the victim has not noticed his enemy's presence or approach is often the result of a more or less clever stratagem of the latter. And even if the attacker's favourable position is a matter of pure chance, as in the case of Galland's first victory over Belgium, the victim's lack of suitable caution can be partly blamed for his predicament. It is not a situation in which the loser has no means of defence, or even attack. He has neglected to use them in the best way. He loses a deadly game at which his adversary is better than he and possibly has more luck, which is part of the game.

Very many ruses are based on the enemy being ignorant of your near presence. The ambush is a classic example. If you scorned to use such a ruse, you would in all conscience have to reject camouflage too! (As the medieval knights undoubtedly would have done.)

Ruses are considered permissible by international law, and are not *per se* contrary to the rules of fair play. It depends on the methods used. A borderline case (as far as fair play is concerned; there was no breach of law) was the "von Eschwege" incident in the First World War.

The German fighter pilot *Leutnant* Rudolf von Eschwege was attached to *Fliegerabteilung 30* at Dráma, on the Macedonian front. He was an intrepid and expert fighter. His Bulgarian allies called him the "Eagle of the Aegean Sea", and both sides respected him for his shrewdness and chivalry. In October and November 1917, with already some 15 victories to his credit, he began playing havoc with the British observation balloons along the front. The commander of 22 Balloon Company,

Major J. Ogilvie Davis, incensed by repeated failures to put a stop to von Eschwege's destruction of his balloons, "resorted to low cunning".[62] He sent up a balloon with in the basket only a dummy observer and 500 lb of explosives, which could be detonated from the ground by means of an electrical circuit. On 21 November 1917 von Eschwege took off in his Albatros D III to attack the balloon, disregarding the objections of his mechanic, who knew that a Bulgarian officer in a forward observation post had reported that he was puzzled by the fact that the British balloon observer was nonchalantly hanging over the basket side and was not moving at all. Von Eschwege climbed and then attacked the balloon in a long, shallow dive. At 50 yards' distance he jerked into a power climb. He may have seen that the observer was only a dummy and have sensed the danger. Anyway, he was too late. Somebody on the ground clicked the switch, blowing up the balloon, destroying the plane and killing von Eschwege. This liquidation of a gallant foe was regarded by most as a sad and shameful act.

The dirty trick that brought von Eschwege down was also used on the Western front, possibly even before November 1917. In his biography of Billy Bishop, a Canadian who, with 72 victories, was the most successful British fighter pilot who survived the First World War, his son tells us that Keith "Grid" Caldwell, "whose wisdom and experience had made him the oldest survivor of 60 Squadron, had warned Bishop that balloons could be 'the nastiest lot of all' ". After describing some of the dangers of attacking a balloon, Caldwell had added: "Always be sure the chaps in the balloon's basket are alive, not dummies. The Hun has a trick of filling the basket with high explosive and detonating it from the ground when you dive in."[63] This warning is supposed to have been given in April 1917, a few weeks after Bishop joined 60 Squadron.

Just one more example will do. In the afternoon of 14 September 1918 a red and white striped Fokker D VII, piloted by *Leutnant* Friedrich Noltenius of *Jasta 11* strafed a British observation balloon near Vis-en-Artois. When he was 150 feet from the balloon, there was a tremendous explosion which severely damaged the Fokker. Noltenius nearly lost control, but managed to reach the German lines. An inspection revealed that the explosion had been more violent than could

Leutnant *Rudolph von Eschwege*.   *(IWM)*

The Canadian ace Billy Bishop in his Nieuport 17 demonstrates the mounting of the Lewis gun on the centre section of the upper wing. The gun had to be hauled back and down to change the ammunition drum, but pilots also used the gun in this position to fire upwards. *(IWM)*

be caused by incendiaries hitting the balloon. "More likely it was a self-destructive 'Eschwege' but Noltenius had no qualms about claiming it as his seventh victory."[64]

Chivalrous behaviour could sometimes produce a humorous situation. In the summer of 1916 the Belgian pilot Edmond Thieffry (later to become an ace) engaged a German fighter pilot in combat. This lasted several minutes, but neither pilot was able to force a decision. They both got off long bursts, without effect. By and by Thieffry exhausted the ammunition in the drum of his Lewis gun. He was flying a Nieuport Bébé, which had its one gun mounted on the upper wing, to fire above the airscrew arc. To reload it, the pilot had to pull the gun back and down and change drums. When Thieffry extended his arm to do this, the German pilot, apparently seeing the outstretched arm and mistaking the gesture for a chivalrous salute, waved back and flew away, leaving Thieffry astonished and alone.[65]

It seems fitting to wind up this chapter on this lighter note. For unless we have set our expectations too high, we can hardly be disappointed, much less depressed, at what we have learned: that most pilots refused to kill an enemy in obvious distress. They — like Lindbergh, who could have killed the man on the beach — will have been grateful for the rest of their lives that they did not kill the defenceless enemy. They will have realized that not taking his life was a much more gentlemanly — and more manly — way to fight than cutting it off.

4

Tributes to the dead

THE death of a gallant adversary will bring no feelings of joy to the heart of a chivalrous fighter. Contentment yes, if he was the one who defeated him in a fair fight. But joy, no. On the contrary, he may be downhearted, and feel regret that the man could not have been brought down alive.

This can only sound paradoxical to those who do not take into account that chivalry implies regarding and treating an honourable adversary with courtesy and respect, recognising him not only as an equal but also as one who belongs to the same international brotherhood of men-at-arms, at the same time being duty-bound to fight him and try to defeat him. In a modern war such an attitude could only be fostered in circumstances we have discussed before, circumstances that were hardly ever found outside the sphere of aerial combat.

The dejection that was felt at the death of an adversary was especially great when respect had grown into admiration. A telling illustration of this is the impact of the death in combat of *Leutnant* Werner Voss on the men who brought him down on 23 September 1917.

At 5 p.m. on that day, 'B' and 'C' Flights of No. 56 Sqn RFC (11 aircraft in all, of the new SE5a type) took off together from their aerodrome at Estrée Blanche, to patrol the front line north-east of Ypres. The two Flights (led by Captains Jimmy McCudden and Geoffrey Bowman) separated but were not far apart. After about an hour McCudden, commanding 'B' Flight, attacked and shot down an artillery observation DFW over Houthem, his 13th victory. But that was not the main

Werner Voss in 1917   *(IWM)*

event of the day. Some 25 minutes later, near Poelcappelle, McCudden sighted an SE5a of No. 60 Sqn being pursued by a Fokker Triplane and getting the worst of it. With Lieutenants Rhys Davids and Cronyn he dived on the Fokker, which let go of his quarry at once and turned on the attackers. These soon got help from Bowman, who had seen what was happening, left the Albatroses he had been engaging, and dived into the fray, accompanied by Lieutenants Hoidge and Maybery. So the lone Fokker was pitted against six SE5as. And they were flown by experienced pilots of an élite squadron; five of them were aces!

But Werner Voss, the pilot of the Fokker, was no ordinary pilot, either. Twenty years of age, he was one of Germany's truly great pilots, a born flyer and also a keen fighter. At the request of Manfred von Richthofen he had been posted to *Jasta 10* on 30 July 1917 to command this *Staffel* of von Richthofen's *Jagdgeschwader Nr. 1*. He had 34 victories to his credit then, and at his throat he proudly wore the *Ordre Pour le Mérite*, in those times Germany's highest award for conspicuous

71

service and gallantry.[1] In August Voss was given one of the two pre-production Fokker Triplanes.[2] "It became his hobby, his pet and indeed his life — his very short life."[3] He especially enjoyed the little plane's extraordinary manoeuvrability. He had it painted a silvery blue and added a frolicsome touch: a face with a moustache was marked on the front of the engine cowling. The 10 victories he won in this plane brought his final tally to 48. Only von Richthofen himself had a higher score, and if any pilot could be expected to better that it was Werner Voss. But on that September evening fate intervened, in the guise of the SE5as of No. 56 Sqn RFC, diving down on him.

Their first attack failed to hit the Fokker which, in the words of McCudden,

> turned in a most disconcertingly quick manner, not a climbing or Immelmann turn, but a sort of flat half spin. By now the German triplane was in the middle of our formation, and its handling was wonderful to behold. The pilot seemed to be firing at all of us simultaneously, and although I got behind him a second time, I could hardly stay there for a second. His movements were so quick and uncertain that none of us could hold him in sight at all for any decisive time.[4]

There were a dozen or more German fighters in the area, but they were prevented from coming to Voss's aid by other Allied planes. Werner Voss fought alone against the deadly British fighters, hemming him in, all trying to get in a position to fire at him. At one time McCudden "noted the triplane in the apex of a cone of tracer bullets from at least five machines simultaneously, and each machine had two guns".[5]

For at least 10 minutes (Rhys Davids reported it as 20!) Werner Voss managed to evade any critical hit. To Maybery he "seemed invulnerable". But it could not last; the odds against him were too great. It was Arthur Rhys Davids who finally shot him down, ending what may well have been the most herioc fight of the war. Only McCudden actually saw the Fokker crash.[6]

When they arrived home, the British officers excitedly discussed the magnificent fight the German pilot had put up. They were all full of praise for him and assumed he must have been one of the enemy's best: von Richthofen, Wolff or Voss. The next morning they got word that it was Voss. Of course

Werner Voss standing in front of his Fokker F.I 103/17, with the white face markings on the cowling. It was in this plane that he met his death on 23 September 1917. (Bundesarchiv)

Rhys Davids was congratulated from all sides, but he expressed everyone's feelings when he said to McCudden: "Oh, if I could only have brought him down alive."[7]

McCudden's combat report erroneously gave the place where Voss had crashed as within the enemy lines. Actually he came down on the Allied side, near St Julian. He was buried with full military honours, a last tribute to a gallant and respected adversary.

But Werner Voss also received tributes in another, more lasting, form from the British pilots who had conquered him. They expressed their great admiration for him in their combat reports. Later McCudden added another tribute, in his book:

> . . . as long as I live I shall never forget my admiration for that German pilot who, single-handed, fought seven of us for ten minutes, and also put some bullets through all of our machines. His flying was wonderful, his courage magnificent, and in my opinion he is the bravest German airman whom it has been my privilege to see fight.[8]

Voss was one of the many — of all services — who were buried with full honours by their enemies, though there was no legal obligation to do more than give them a decent burial. The

73

Geneva "Convention on the wounded and sick"* that was in force in the First World War (the 1906 version, adapted to maritime warfare by a Hague Convention in 1907) enjoined the belligerents to make a careful examination of the bodies of the dead, prior to their burial (whether by land or sea) or cremation. That was all. The next version of this Convention, signed in 1929, and thus in force in the Second World War, added: "They shall further ensure that the dead are honourably interred, that their graves are respected and marked so that they may always be found."

Often much more was done, on both sides, to pay homage to the enemy dead. In this respect, again, the air forces particularly distinguished themselves, especially in the First World War. The military honours usually included most (sometimes all) of the following: the coffin was carried to the hearse and escorted to the cemetery by a bearer party of the dead man's military peers, a funeral service was read at the graveside, volleys were fired over the grave, the Last Post was sounded by buglers, and wreaths and flowers were laid on the grave. In some cases one or more aircraft flew overhead and dipped in a salute.[9]

A funeral that had all those elements was that of Manfred Freiherr von Richthofen, in the late afternoon of 22 April 1918, at the cemetery of the small French village of Bertangles, some five miles north of Amiens. A detailed description of his burial, with several photographs, is given in Bruce Robertson (Ed.), *Von Richthofen and the Flying Circus* (1958). Remarkably, this account does not mention that "overhead there waved a flight of aeroplanes paying their tribute of respect", as Hamilton Fyfe reported in the *Daily Mail* of 24 April 1918.

The next day, a British pilot flew low over the aerodrome at Cappy, from where von Richthofen had taken off for his last flight. He dropped a container with a streamer attached. In it was a photograph of the funeral and the following message:

TO THE GERMAN FLYING CORPS

Rittmeister Baron Manfred von Richthofen was killed in aerial combat on April 21, 1918. He was buried with full military honours.

From the BRITISH ROYAL AIR FORCE[10]

* Strangely enough, the dead are not mentioned in the name of the Convention, although it comprises injunctions concerning them.

Funeral of Manfred von Richthofen at Bertangles on 22 April 1918. Officers of 3 Sqn Australian Flying Corps lower the coffin into the grave.   *(IWM)*

The people at home did not always understand why homage should be paid to enemies of their country. Some were furious. In a letter in the *Daily Mail* of 4 May 1918 a lady protested against "the awful insult we have suffered by seeing in the daily papers pictures of glorious spring flowers made into wreaths being held over the grave of von Richthofen, a low, murderous Boche". She got a quick response in the columns of the newspaper from correspondents who commented that the officers of the RAF were the best judges in such a matter, and that, in their opinion, von Richthofen was a gallant man, a sportsman and a clean fighter.

But to be honest, those who objected to honouring fallen enemies could hardly be blamed for not being able to enter into the mentality of the military men who considered it their honourable duty. The gap between them was indeed very wide. At best the objectors saw the elaborate ceremonies as injudicious playing with matters that were too grim for that. (After all, what did they know of the play element in culture?)

At worst they regarded those honours as humbug, as disgusting hypocrisy, or even as a treason to their own dead.

75

The burial with military honours of the crews of the German airships shot down on their bombing raids over Britain was a special affront to many. These Germans had been killing civilians and, however brave they might have been, they certainly could not be called fair fighters. "Baby killers" was the epithet universally used for the Zeppelin airmen.

When on 6 September 1916 the 16-member crew of the German airship SL 11* was buried with full honours at Potters Bar, police were out in force to prevent any disturbances of the proceedings by the crowd that had gathered near the cemetery, to which only parishioners were admitted, The only incident occurred when "as the coffins were being borne through the gates a middle-aged woman threw two eggs at one of them, which spattered on the black shroud covering it".[11] During the funeral a RFC pilot flew overhead, in a BE2c, the same type of aeroplane as the one with which Lieutenant William Leefe Robinson of No. 39 (Home Defence) Sqn had shot down SL 11 three days before.[12] Two days later Robinson received the Victoria Cross from the hands of HM King George V, at Windsor Castle.

Considering the emotional protests of civilians against the military honours paid to dead enemy airmen in the First World War — a war in which the suffering of the population at the hands of the air forces was as nothing compared with what it had to endure 25 years later — one would have expected a far stronger outcry against such honours in the Second World War. But, unless much care was taken to suppress or tone down reports of incidents, this was not the case, on either side. There were complaints, though, even occasioning a question in the House of Commons, on 3 June 1943. Sir Archibald Sinclair, the Secretary of State for Air, replied:

> The body of a German airman was found on the foreshore at Burnham-on-Sea on 24 May and was buried with Service honours at Weston-super-Mare on 27 May in accordance with the obligations of His Majesty's Government under the Geneva Convention. The burial took place in a section of the cemetery reserved for Service personnel which is some 200-300 yards from the nearest civilian graves. Enemy dead have previously been interred in this plot.[13]

* The letters SL stood for Schütte-Lanz. Though airships of this make were commonly called Zeppelins, too, strictly speaking this was not correct.

Apparently a distance of 200-300 yards was considered safe, in death.

Whether Sir Archibald was right in citing the Geneva Convention depends on the interpretation of the words "honourably interred" of the Convention*. They need not necessarily mean "with (full) military honours".

Particularly in the First World War, the air forces often availed themselves of the unique opportunity they had to communicate rapidly and with more than just words with the enemy, that is by dropping messages and other (harmless) things on his airfields or elsewhere in the enemy lines. When Lieutenant von Eschwege was killed on the Macedonian front**, the RFC dropped a message:

> To the Bulgarian-German Flying Corps in Drama. The officers of the Royal Flying Corps regret to announce that Lieut. von Eschwege was killed while attacking the captive balloon. His personal belongings will be dropped over the lines some time during the next few days.[14]

On the following day a German aeroplane dropped a wreath, a flag and a letter addressed to the RFC. The letter read (in part):

> We thank you sincerely for your information regarding our comrade Lieut. von Eschwege, and request you to permit the accompanying wreath and flag to be placed on his last resting place.   *DEUTSCHES FLIEGERKOMMANDO.*[15]

In their turn again, the RFC dropped von Eschwege's personal effects, together with photographs of his burial.

About three weeks earlier, on the same front (which had a reputation for chivalrous behaviour by both sides), the British were notified of the death in aerial combat of 2nd Lieutenant P. D. Montague, through a message dropped by an enemy aeroplane. It was written in Bulgarian, and translated it ran:

> On the 29th of October 1917 one of your comrades met with a hero's death in an air fight. He was buried with due honours, and a memorial stone has been put up over his grave, but without an inscription, as his name is not known to us. In order that we may make good this deficiency, kindly

* See p. 73
** See p. 68

77

inform us as to his name and the date and place of his birth. The reply should be addressed to 'Bulgarian Airmen'.[16]

In most cases the inscription on the gravestone or cross gave no more than the name, rank and dates of birth and death of the adversary buried there. On occasion, however, a few words were added, expressing respect and admiration for a gallant foe. Words like those carved by a German Grenadier on the makeshift cross over the provisional grave of one of Britain's greatest air fighters in the First World War, Major L. G. Hawker, VC, DSO: *Gefallen nach heldenhaftem Luftkampf* (Fallen after heroic air combat).

When Major Lanoe George Hawker took off from Bertangles aerodrome on 23 November 1916, for his last flight, he had been Commanding Officer of 24 Squadron, the RFC's first single-seat scout (fighter) unit, for more than a year. Before that he had served in 6 Sqn, and during that time he had first been awarded the Distinguished Service Order and then his country's highest military decoration, the Victoria Cross. Not only was he a skilled, courageous and resourceful air fighter, he also made an important contribution to forming the rules and tactics of aerial combat and introduced numerous technical innovations. Soon he also proved to be a great leader of men; his subordinates were absolutely devoted to him.

As squadron commander Hawker was officially forbidden to fly across the lines with his men, but he disregarded that order and often joined a patrol, sometimes substituting himself for another pilot at the last moment. On 23 November 1916 he attached himself to 'A' Flight when it started out on an early afternoon patrol. The four De Havilland DH2s took off at 1 p.m., but shortly one of them had to land with engine trouble. Captain Andrews led the patrol, Hawker flew on his left and Lieutenant Saundby* on his right. After about an hour they engaged a couple of German two-seaters north-east of Bapaume. Andrews broke off the attack when he discovered that they were decoys for two groups of Albatros fighters flying higher up. Hawker, however, continued to dive after the two-seaters. He got separated from the two others, who last saw him fighting an Albatros D II at about 3000 feet.

And what a fight it was! The Albatros was flown by none

* Later Air Marshal Sir Robert Saundby, KCB, KBE, MC, DFC, AFC, DL.

Major Lanoe George Hawker, VC, DSO, who was killed on 23 November 1916 in an epic duel with Manfred von Richthofen. **(IWM)**

other than Manfred von Richthofen. Two great air fighters had met and started a duel that was to last 35 minutes. Hawker was at a considerable disadvantage. The Albatros D II was greatly superior to the DH2. It was much faster, had a better rate of climb, and had two machine-guns against only one on the DH2. The sole advantage the British machine had was that it could turn more sharply. There was another circumstance that weighed the odds still more heavily against Hawker: they were fighting well over the German side of the lines and there was a westerly wind which drifted them steadily further into German-held territory. Sooner or later Hawker would have to break off the fight and try to race back across the lines, unless, of course, he chose to land and give himself up as a prisoner-of-war — an unthinkable alternative to a determined fighter like him. Breaking off the fight would mean giving his adversary a deadly firing position on his tail, an almost suicidal manoeuvre in his slower aircraft, and one that had to be postponed as long as possible.

The duellists circled round and round, each trying to get behind and above the other, to attain a shooting position. Twenty circles to the left, then 30 to the right. "The circles we made round one another," wrote von Richthofen, "were so narrow that I estimated their diameter at no more than 250 or 300 feet. I had time to take a good look at my opponent. I looked straight down into his fuselage and could observe every movement of his head. If he had not worn his cap, I would have been able to tell the expression on his face."[17] Once Hawker actually waved to von Richthofen.

But the sands were running out. Hawker had to make a break for it. After some sudden and violent manoeuvres to try and distract his adversary, he dived away towards the trenches, zig-zagging close to the ground to make a difficult target. Von Richthofen fired short bursts at him, but scored no hits. And then, dramatically, both the German's guns jammed, and it seemed as if Hawker would escape after all. But von Richthofen managed to get one gun firing again and one bullet of his next burst hit Hawker in the head. His machine crashed into the shell-ravaged area 2¼ miles south of Bapaume, very near the British lines, which he would have reached in a matter of seconds. Von Richthofen had nearly exhausted his ammunition;

he had already fired 900 rounds. Only one of these hit. One was enough.

The exciting duel between the two aces had been witnessed by the German Major von Schönberg of the 100th Royal Saxon Reserve Grenadier Regiment and many of his men. They also saw Hawker crash 250 yards from the ruins of a farm which served them as a shelter. As the area was under fire from British machine-guns, they could not go to the wreck.

> The next morning Lieut. Bergmann reported to Major von Schönberg that the English officer was still lying under the wrecked aeroplane, and asked if he might bury him. Major von Schönberg gladly granted this permission and said that such a brave enemy should be accorded the honours due to him. Lanoe was buried beside his fallen machine.
>
> Major von Schönberg's batman, Grenadier Paul Fischer, made a cross from the wreckage of the aeroplane, carved an inscription upon it, and placed it over the grave:
>
> "HIER RUHT DER ENGLISCHE MAJOR HAWKER
> VOM BRITISH ROYAL FLYING CORPS,
> GEFALLEN NACH HELDENHAFTEM LUFTKAMPF
> Am 23.11.16"
>
> Thus in the noblest traditions of military chivalry, these courteous and kindly Saxons, in spite of their intense sufferings during the Battle of the Somme, paid military honours to their fallen foe.[18]

It was not only airmen that upheld the ideals of chivalry!

Von Richthofen was extremely proud when he was informed that the man he had brought down was the well-known Major Hawker. "According to prisoners' accounts he was the English Boelcke," he wrote to his mother two days later.

Von Richthofen was in the habit of collecting pieces from the wreckage of the aeroplanes he had shot down, as trophies. Sometimes he fetched them personally, in other cases this was done for him. From Hawker's machine he received a piece of fabric with the serial number of the aeroplane (5964) and its Lewis gun. Like all his trophies they ended up adorning the walls of his bedroom at his mother's home at Schweidnitz* in Silesia. The machine-gun from Hawker's plane got pride of place, over the entrance door.

* Nowadays a Polish place, named Świdnica.

Von Richthofen also had another collection of trophies. For each of his victories he had a Berlin jeweller make a small silver cup (about two inches high) and inscribe it with the number of the victory, the type of the enemy plane, whether it was a single- or two-seater, and the date. The cup for his victory over Hawker (his 11th) was inscribed "11. Vickers 1. 23.11.16". It is strange that he should have misidentified Hawker's plane, as it is known that he had inspected a captured DH2 the previous September,[19] and all Vickers aircraft then operational which resembled the DH2 (a pusher-plane) were two-seaters.

According to Floyd Gibbons, von Richthofen

> personally dropped a note from the air behind the English lines, addressed to Hawker's comrades of the Royal Flying Corps, stating briefly the death of the English ace and expressing the widespread admiration of German airmen for him as an exceptionally brave airman and a chivalrous foe.[20]

If so, the note never reached its destination. In a letter to Lanoe Hawker's mother, dated 28 November 1916, Brigadier-General E. B. Ashmore, Commanding 4th Brigade, RFC (under whose command 24 Sqn operated), told her that her son was missing and that there was a good chance of his being a prisoner. "We have dropped messages to ask for news, but the Germans do not often give us information now . . .".

Seeing that the dropping of messages to the enemy is so frequently mentioned in narratives on the First World War*, the lack of communication in the case of Hawker's death is remarkable. From Brigadier-General Ashmore's regretful comment it would seem that some of those stories might be exaggerated, or even made up, as Floyd Gibbons' version appears to be. Anyhow, it was not until July 1917 that definite news of Hawker's death was received from Germany.[21]

Gibbons also writes that

> Richthofen's flying mates arranged a military funeral for their fallen foe, but the man who brought him down did not attend the ceremonies, which was according to the custom then in vogue.[22]

I cannot comment on the custom he refers to; I have not found

* See also chapter 5.

it mentioned anywhere else. But it is highly unlikely that the ceremonies took place at all! One cannot think of a reason why Tyrrel Mann Hawker, Lanoe's brother, who wrote the biography quoted earlier, would fail to include them in his book. He does tell of Lanoe's burial by German Grenadiers on the spot where he fell. There is even a photograph (of bad quality, but undoubtedly authentic) of the wreck of the plane, with two Germans standing beside it and the cross over his grave visible in the background. He remains silent on what subsequently happened to his brother's remains. It must have been too distasteful to him to write that the area was so much devastated by the battles fluctuating over it that his brother's body could not be found again in order to be reburied. That this is what happened can be deduced from his description (dated 23 November 1936, 20 years after Lanoe's death) of the Air Services Memorial at a cemetery at Arras. On the four sides of the obelisk are inscribed the names of the missing of the Royal Flying Corps, the Royal Naval Air Service, the Royal Air Force* and the air services of the Dominions respectively. Lanoe Hawker's name heads the list of the *missing* of the Royal Flying Corps. "So in the company of some of the lads he loved and inspired with his great courage Lanoe's name is engraved for all to see."[23]

The burials I have described so far were of airmen whose bodies had been recovered by their enemies, who laid them to rest with ceremonies that testified their sense of honour and, on occasion, their admiration for the courage and skill their adversary had shown. Sometimes — as in the case of von Eschwege — the dead man's comrades, unable to attend the funeral, delivered their token of mourning, to be placed on the grave in the hostile ground. But they were not often in a position to pay their last respects in this way.

Naturally, when those who had fallen were buried by their own side, by their companions in arms, there was no want of honours and mourners at their funerals. What made some of these funerals in the First World War remarkable, however, was that the enemy felt in honour bound to have a share in the homage paid, and found a way of delivering a mark of their

* The RAF was formed on 1 April 1918 (more than seven months before the end of the First World War) by the amalgamation of the RFC and the RNAS.

respect, usually in the form of a wreath. References to the dropping of wreaths in token of respect for a gallant adversary are fairly frequently found in books dealing with the First World War. Some writers even say that it was customary,[24] which is probably an exaggeration. But it was certainly done at the deaths of Pégoud, Immelmann and Boelcke, three famous names in the history of the air war.

The Frenchman Adolphe Pégoud was already a famous aviator before the First World War broke out. He had learned to fly during his military service (as a mechanic, not officially), and after his discharge from the service he was set upon making a career in aviation. Early in 1913 he landed a job with Louis Blériot, who had won fame by crossing the Channel in an aeroplane for the first time in 1909, and now had a factory for the production of the aeroplanes he designed. Pégoud became what later would be called a factory test pilot.

Within a few months he had taken a spectacular share in the series of impressive aviation enterprises in 1913 that made French historians refer to that year as *La Glorieuse Année*. In August he successfully demonstrated a Bonnet parachute by jumping with it from an old expendable aeroplane he had taken up himself. It was the first parachute jump from an aeroplane in Europe. It is said that watching the behaviour of the then pilotless plane, he decided that he would next experiment with upside-down flying. Two weeks later, at Juvisy aerodrome, he gave a demonstration of inverted flight that caused a sensation.

Pégoud had an even greater thrill in store for the public. On 21 September 1913, over Buc aerodrome near Versailles, he astonished the spectators by looping the loop. He was not the first aviator to accomplish this feat, though. Peter Nesterov, a lieutenant in the Imperial Russian Air Force, had beaten him to that distinction by a month, performing a loop in a Nieuport aeroplane on 20 August, at Kiev. (His superiors were less than enthusiastic, charged him with endangering government property, and placed him under house arrest for a month.[25]) But Pégoud is generally — and deservedly — regarded as the creator of aerobatics. Only a few days after his first loop he started on an extensive tour of Europe, during which his spectacular flying displays profoundly impressed both the lay public and his

Adolphe Pégoud (right) with a passenger and a couple of curious onlookers at Johannisthal, near Berlin, during his tour of Europe in 1913.   (Bundesarchiv)

fellow aviators, who were left in no doubt of his unique mastery of the new art. Pégoud's displays were by no means limited to upside down flying and loops. At Brooklands, at the end of September, he also performed a vertical S (a bunt* followed by half a loop), a tailslide and — incredibly — a complete outside loop.[26]

His tour brought Pégoud into contact with dozens of aviators of different nationalities. He had become an important member of the international brotherhood of early conquerors of the air, many of whom found themselves fighting each other in the air a year later.

In the war that broke out in 1914 Adolphe Pégoud served his country as a pilot, of course, in the *Aviation Militaire*. He became the first man to have shot down five enemy aeroplanes. And as this was quite a number in that first year of aerial warfare, the French press called him *un As* (Ace, the highest of

* A manoeuvre in which an aeroplane performs half an outside loop downwards and emerges upside down going in the opposite direction.

a set of cards), which was current sports slang in France, meaning "champion". Thus, five victories became the fortuitous standard by which one qualified as an ace,[27] an appellation soon to be used in the official French communiqués as well.

Sous-Lieutenant Pégoud added one more victory to his score before, on 31 August 1915, he met his death over Belfort (Alsace). Flying a Morane-Saulnier Type N monoplane of *Escadrille MS.49,* he attacked a German observation plane that was entering French air space. The German gunner's return fire killed Pégoud with a bullet through his heart. His machine dived down from 10,000 feet and crashed. Two days later the crew of the German plane that had shot him down (Kandulski and von Bilitz) dropped a wreath on the site of the crash, inscribed *Den im Kampfe für sein Vaterland gefallenen Flieger Pégoud ehrt der Gegner* (The aviator Pégoud fallen in combat for his country, is honoured by his adversary).[28] A second wreath was also dropped by the Germans, this one with an inscription in French: *A Pégoud, mort en héros, son adversaire.*[29]

At the time Pégoud was killed, Max Immelmann had just started on a meteoric career as a fighter pilot in the German Air Service. After some combat experience on armed two-seaters, he had, in May 1915, joined the recently formed *Feldfliegerabteilung 62,** at Douai.

Immelmann was not popular with the other men. His ascetic way of life and his stuffiness caused wonder and irritation. He was a non-smoker, a teetotaller, a vegetarian, and had no interest at all in women. It is improbable that one could find anybody so much different from the typical aviator that he was. But he was a fine pilot. Notwithstanding an earlier reputation for making bad landings that caused a lot of damage, he is later described as an exceptionally gifted pilot.

One of the other pilots in *Feldfliegerabteilung 62* was Oswald Boelcke, also destined to become one of Germany's prominent aces. In fact, his and Immelmann's fighting careers were strikingly similar. Their victory scores went up at the same rate and they were awarded the *Pour le Mérite* on the same day, 12

---

* The *Feldfliegerabteilungen* (lit.: sections of flyers for the field) were the most important units of the German Air Service before this was reorganized later in the war.

Feldfliegerabteilung 62, *Douai, 20 January 1916. In centre, from left to right, Boelcke, Hauptmann Kastner (the CO) and Immelmann.* *(IWM)*

January 1916. Often flying in company, they together moulded new successful tactics of aerial combat. They owed much of their success to a new type of aeroplane that Anthony Fokker, a Dutchman building planes for the Germans, came up with in May 1915, the Fok. E I (E for *Eindecker*, monoplane), a small single-seat fighter. Despite its rather poor performance, the E I, soon to be followed by the improved E II, E III and E IV, proved to be a deadly weapon in the hands of skilled pilots like Boelcke and Immelmann, not least because the *Eindeckers* were armed with a machine-gun** that could be fired through the propeller arc.

Early in June Fokker arrived at Douai with two E Is, to familiarise the pilots of the several *Feldfliegerabteilungen* based there with his new plane. "At Fl. Abt. 62 Fokker selected *Leut.* Boelcke for tuition. When Fokker departed after a stay of about two weeks he left one of his demonstration aircraft (E 3/15) with Boelcke."[30] In the E I a passenger could be squeezed in behind the pilot and Boelcke made good use of

** The E III could have two guns; the E IV had two. One special E IV for Immelmann even had three.

this "to give brother officers, mechanics and pretty nurses their baptism of flying in a single-seat fighter."[31]

On 30 July, Immelmann was taken up by Boelcke for one instruction flight. After that he was allowed to make a few solo flights.[32] Then, surprisingly, it was Immelmann who scored the first victory won by a Fokker monoplane, on 1 August 1915. It was also his first personal victory. He had the "colossal luck", wrote Boelcke in a letter,[33] to catch an unarmed British plane that was bombing Douai aerodrome. He damaged the plane and wounded the pilot, who was compelled to land. Immelmann immediately landed beside him and walked towards him, shouting that he was a prisoner. The enemy pilot, a Lieutenant William Reid, made a gesture of surrender, whereupon Immelmann shook hands with him and said, "Bonjour, monsieur", being for some reason under the impression that his adversary was French. When the answer proved otherwise, a short conversation in English followed. Lieutenant Reid told him his arm was broken, adding courteously, "You shot very well".[34]

Meetings like this, after a fight, between conqueror and conquered, characterized by congeniality and courtesy, occurred fairly frequently in the First World War and were not uncommon in the Second either. Chapter 6 of this book deals with them.

The appearance of the Fokker E-planes over the Western Front heralded a period of success for the German Air Service. The aggressive little fighter planes with their efficient armament gave the French and the British a most unpleasant surprise, soon turning to consternation when they began to inflict really heavy losses on the Allied aircraft. In reporting this turn of events, the Allied press showed little wisdom and restraint, and grossly exaggerated the reverses suffered by their air forces. The British press spoke of the 'Fokker Scourge', and in March 1916 a Member of Parliament, sharply criticising the quality of British-built aeroplanes, said that they were no more than 'Fokker fodder'.

All this was, of course, most welcome to the Germans, as it undermined Allied morale. They did not neglect to add fanciful details to the actual facts. As 'super pilots' flying the *Eindeckers,* two in particular were publicized: Boelcke and

The note attached to the wreath dropped by an RFC crew over the enemy lines after Immelmann's death (see page 90). Note the mis-spelt name.

(Bundesarchiv)

Immelmann, not indeed without justification. Immelmann was called *Der Adler von Lille* (The Eagle of Lille), and some legends were woven round his person. For instance, it was said that he was one of the pilots who, in mid-August 1914, dropped the leaflets on Paris in which the citizens were exhorted to surrender since the Germans were at the gates. But Immelmann could not yet even fly at that time! Also there is an apocryphal story (which, however, by its nature ought not to be left out of this book) that Immelmann was once seen to say a prayer in the open field by the dead body of an adversary he had shot down.[35]

The names of Immelmann and Boelcke became well known on the Allied side, too, as a kind of 'terrible twins' (actually they were of nearly the same age). There were quite a few instances in which an Allied pilot, after coming down on the German side, having lost but survived an aerial combat, was mollified on hearing that his conqueror was Immelmann or Boelcke.[36] It was no disgrace to be defeated by such a famous ace!

One gets the impression that until the middle of 1916 Immelmann was the better known of the two. Possibly because his name was associated with a specific combat manoeuvre he introduced: the 'Immelmann turn'.[37]

On the evening of 18 June 1916 Max Immelmann (25 years old, after 15 victories) was killed in combat with FE2bs of 25 Sqn RFC. His Fokker E III was seen to rear itself up, dive away and then break up. It has never become clear what caused his fall. The RFC claimed he fell to the guns of Corporal J. H. Waller, the gunner of the FE2b piloted by 2nd Lieutenant G. R. McCubbin. The Germans on the other hand were convinced that owing to a malfunction of his interrupter gear* Immelmann shot away one of the blades of his own propeller, and that the resulting excessive vibration made it impossible for him to control the plane and prevent its breaking up.

On 22 June, Immelmann's body lay in state in the courtyard of the hospital at Douai, surrounded by wreaths and roses in profusion. Princes, generals and deputations of all units of the German Air Service were among the numerous mourners for the fallen hero.

The Royal Flying Corps honoured the man who had inflicted such painful losses on its airmen, but had always been a gallant

---

* The mechanism that enabled the machine-gun(s) to be fired through the revolving propeller.

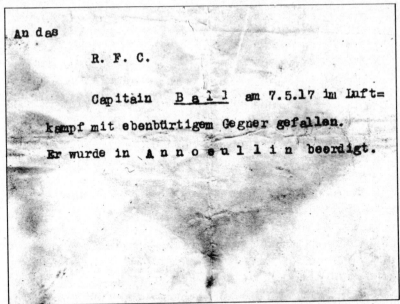

Message dropped by the Germans to announce the death of the British ace Albert Ball. Translation: To the R.F.C. Captain Ball killed on 7.5.17 in aerial combat with an adversary equal to him. He was buried in Annoeullin.   (IWM)

and chivalrous adversary, by dropping a funeral wreath by parachute over the enemy lines. This was done by Allister M. Miller, a South African pilot, and his observer, with a note which read: "To the memory of Ltn. Immelmann, our brave and chivalrous opponent, from the British Royal Flying Corps." Attached to this was a note in Miller's own hand:

> We have come over to drop this wreath as a tribute of the respect the British Flying Corps held for Leiut. Immelman. We consider it an honour to have been detailed for this special work. Lt. Immelman was respected by all British airmen, one and all agreeing that he was a thorough sportsman.[38]

It seems that several squadrons followed suit and delivered wreaths of their own, sometimes at great risk to the men who dropped them.[39] After the ceremonies at Douai, Immelmann's body was taken by train to Dresden, his native town, for the funeral.

During a visit to Germany in 1932, Captain D. Leeson, a Canadian who — as the observer of a BE2c of 16 Sqn — had been shot down by Immelmann on 10 October 1915 and been taken prisoner, laid a wreath on his former opponent's grave in Dresden.[40]

A strong case could be made out for rating Oswald Boelcke the greatest ace of the First World War. That is to say, if it were agreed that the number of enemy planes a pilot shot down cannot reasonably be the only criterion of deciding his rating, not even if one took into consideration the period of the war and the span of time in which his victories were won. Leadership, personal courage and chivalry should also carry weight.[41]

Boelcke outlived Immelmann by about 4½ months. Nearly half of that time it was not possible for him to win new victories in the air. At the end of June 1916, by order of the Emperor himself, he was forbidden to fly. He had become too important to the German Air Service to expose him to the dangers of aerial combat any longer. Not only because he was an idol of the German people, whose loss, after Immelmann's death, would be another blow to morale, but also — perhaps more — because Boelcke had proved to be an outstanding leader and teacher, and had become an authority on aerial tactics.

Predictably, Boelcke was greatly annoyed at being grounded. By way of consolation he was sent on an inspection tour to Turkey, which pleased him. But before his departure he spent a few days at Charleville with Major Hermann Thomsen, *Chef des Feldflugwesens* (Chief of Field Aviation), and his staff. They discussed the further development of that new branch of military aviation: the fighter arm, which was to be organized in *Jagdstaffeln*. Boelcke contributed his knowledge, experience and views, and brought his methodical mind to bear on solving the organizational problems that arose. It was during those days that Boelcke, at the request of Thomsen, wrote down his basic tactical rules of air fighting. These nine rules, sometimes called the *Boelcke Dicta*,[42] have retained their validity, not only to the end of the First World War, but also throughout the Second, and even in later conflicts.

Boelcke travelled to Turkey by way of Austria, and on the return journey visited Bulgaria and the Russian Front. Here he interviewed several pilots, with a view to finding good men for his new *Jagdstaffel* on the Western Front. He chose the young

Oswald Boelcke (middle, wearing the Pour le Mérite) *at the German General HQ at Charleville, summer 1916, the time he formulated the "Boelcke Dicta".*
(IWM)

lieutenant Manfred von Richthofen, whom he remembered from an earlier chance meeting in a dining-car of a train, and the much older lieutenant Erwin Böhme (37). Von Richthofen became his most brilliant pupil, Böhme his closest friend.

During Boelcke's six weeks' absence from the Western Front, the British had launched the Battle of the Somme and attained local air superiority. The Germans were unable to check the British reconnaissance and artillery planes, with disastrous consequences for the ground troops. Boelcke was urgently recalled from his tour, to re-establish and lead the fighter unit he had been building up before his departure. It officially became *Jagdstaffel 2* on 27 August 1916, based at Bertincourt, but there were no aeroplanes yet. The first two arrived on 1 September, one Albatros and one Fokker D III, in which Boelcke scored his 20th victory the next day. In the next eight weeks, the last heroic weeks of his life, he won another 20 victories. No other pilot of any nationality had won more than Boelcke when he died.

Boelcke won his 20th victory by forcing down a De Havilland DH2 west of Bapaume, on the German side of the lines. The British pilot, Captain R. E. Wilson, of 23 Sqn RFC, had come to the rescue of a BE2e artillery plane that was being attacked, and he got into serious difficulties when he was engaged by Boelcke. He was no match for the German ace and his plane was so severely damaged that he had to crash-land it. It burst into flames, but Wilson, who was unhurt, managed to jump out in time and throw off his coat, which had caught fire. Boelcke flew low over his victim, to observe the situation, and then left the scene. The next day, 3 September, he called for Captain Wilson at the POW transit camp, took him to his aerodrome and showed him round. They had coffee together in the mess, and Boelcke drew a great deal of interesting information out of Wilson.[43]

Robert Wilson has written about his meeting with Boelcke that his adversary had made a deep impression on him. Not only because he was such a splendid pilot, but also because of his strong personality. He also wrote that his combat with Boelcke, even if it had an unfavourable outcome for him, would remain his life's greatest memory.[44]

In the same month of September Boelcke had a meeting in the air with a colourful French personality, Paul Tarascon, who was to end the First World War with 12 victories and to take up arms against the German invaders of his country again in the next World War, not as a pilot this time, but as a member of the French Resistance. They duelled over the Somme, Boelcke in an Albatros, Tarascon in a Nieuport. In this fight, which lasted seven or eight minutes, both pilots exhausted their ammunition.

> Each time one was set up for a killing burst, the other managed to whip away with some astonishing manoeuvre. 'I can still see the black leather helmet of Boelcke' — Tarascon's favourite recollection — 'as I crossed him like a flash and he tossed me a sporting salute.'
>
> With ammunition gone, there was nothing to do but to wave. Tarascon and Boelcke, calling it a draw, headed home.

Wreath and message dropped by the RFC at the death of Boelcke.

(Bundesarchiv)

> 'It is with great pleasure that, in a sense of sportsmanship, I render homage to the great aviator that was Boelcke.
>
> 'Our combat was without mercy, for Honour, but of such dignity, such a knightlyness, that, if our combat had been favourable to me, I would have solicited for him, for this knight of the air, privileged treatment.'[45]

To Boelcke, the adversaries he met in the air and occasionally on the ground, as prisoners, were honourable foes, worthy of courtesy and respect. He disliked the disparaging remarks that German newspapers sometimes made about the Allied airmen. He once countered with the statement, "The Englishman is brave and tough; a sportsman."[46]

Reading Boelcke's letters, one is repeatedly struck by the zest for fighting that they reveal. For example, a combat with a British two-seater west of Cambrai on New Year's Eve 1915, in which Immelmann was also involved, is described in these terms: "That was a beautiful fight. I was having to do with a tough customer, who defended himself bravely." And, after relating how the adversary escaped, "Smart fellow! It is not everyone who could do that. Well, it was not a victory, but nevertheless a lusty fight!"[47]

It is sometimes said that the bravest men are those who know fear but are able to master it when meeting danger. By this criterion, Boelcke did not belong to that category: from all accounts he was one of those rare men who are completely fearless. Also by his own account. Without conceit, almost apologetically, he more than once writes in letters to his parents that fortunately he does not know what nerves are, that he is fearless.

Such then is the image of *Hauptmann* Oswald Boelcke at the time of his death, at the age of 25: a master pilot, an eager, brave and successful fighter, a great tactician, a beloved leader, a chivalrous man, greatly honoured by everyone, friend or foe.

Boelcke died on a dreary autumn day, 28 October 1916. He had already flown five missions that day and he and his pilots were tired. He had just begun a game of chess with his good friend Erwin Böhme, when the *Staffel* was once again called to the front. They took off and soon met and engaged two DH2s of 24 Sqn RFC*, over Flers. Dog-fighting developed, at one stage of which Boelcke and Böhme were chasing one of the British machines between them when the other, pursued by von Richthofen, crossed their line of flight, so that they both had to swerve to avoid crashing into it. Momentarily they lost sight of one another and their aircraft collided. Böhme's undercarriage struck Boelcke's upper wing, fatally damaging it. The others watched Boelcke's Albatros spiral down. At first it seemed as if Boelcke would succeed in keeping control over his machine, but when he got into some squalls he lost it, crashed, and was killed outright.

Böhme wanted to land near the scene of the crash, but the trenches and shell holes that covered the area made that impossible. He flew back to their airfield, overturning his plane on landing. Böhme was inconsolable and only slowly recovered from the emotional shock of having been instrumental in causing his friend's death, although he was fully aware of the fact that he was in no way to blame. In a letter to his girlfriend we find the despairing cry, "Why did he, the irreplaceable,

---

* The squadron commanded by Major Lanoe Hawker (see earlier), who did not take part in the fight himself, however. The DH2s were flown by Lieutenants Knight and McKay.[48]

have to be the victim of this blind fate, and why not I?"[49] Erwin
Böhme was one of the later commanders of *Jasta Boelcke,* in
which function he was killed in action over Flanders on 29
November 1917, one year, one month and one day after
Boelcke died.

The grand ceremonies that preceded and attended Boelcke's
funeral reflected the idolisation of their national hero by the
German people and the depth of their feelings of loss.

On 31 October, after an impressive memorial service in the
large cathedral of Cambrai, the coffin was taken to the railway
station on a gun-carriage drawn by six black horses. In front
strode Manfred von Richthofen, bearing the cushion with
Boelcke's decorations. Aeroplanes were flying overhead. At
the station, in front of the railway van in which Boelcke's body
was to be transported to Germany, the coffin was once more
placed on a bier. General von Below, commander of the *I.
Armee,* and representing the Emperor, delivered a funeral
oration. After him *Oberleutnant* Kirmaier, Boelcke's immediate
successor as commanding officer of *Jasta 2,* spoke. A volley
was fired over the coffin, which was then placed in the draped
van, together with the many flowers and wreaths that had been
sent to honour the fallen hero. The train, in which Boelcke's
parents, three brothers and a sister travelled, too, carried him
to Dessau, his home town. On 2 November he was buried
there. Thousands upon thousands lined the streets to the
cemetery south of the town. Both in the funeral orations and in
the reports on Boelcke's death and burial it was repeatedly
stressed that he had been killed in an accident, that he
remained undefeated by the enemy until the end.[50]

Among the wreaths that were received there were two from
his adversaries. One had been dropped by the RFC, with a
typed note:

> TO THE MEMORY OF CAPTAIN BOELKE, OUR
> BRAVE AND CHIVALROUS OPPONENT.
> FROM, THE ENGLISH ROYAL FLYING CORPS.[51]

The other wreath had been sent by four English pilots who
were prisoners-of-war in Osnabrück, dedicated to their "highly
admired and honoured adversary". One of these four was
Captain Wilson, who had been brought down by Boelcke two
months before.

I have dealt at some length with three cases in which funeral wreaths were dropped or otherwise delivered by the enemy, to do homage to a greatly respected adversary. All three concerned a famous man and that is why they are so well documented.

That there were — in the First World War — more such cases, can be gathered from an occasional reference to this particular form of tribute. For example, Erwin Böhme writes to his fiancée in a letter dated 7 November 1917:

> More and more a really chivalrous custom has developed between us and the English pilots: we inform each other — by messages which, attached to small sandbags, are dropped at the camps — of what has happened to those who are missing, we also drop funeral wreaths for those who have fallen.[52]

But it is unlikely that wreaths were dropped many times, or one would have found it mentioned more often.

I know of only one instance in the Second World War of a wreath being dropped to do honour to a fallen adversary. This was dispatched by Air Commodore R. Collishaw, when his opponent in North Africa, the Italian Air Marshal Italo Balbo*, was shot down by his own anti-aircraft guns over Tobruk on 28 June 1940.[53] It was a kind of throwback to the more chivalrous times of the 1914-1918 war, when Raymond Collishaw was a most successful fighter pilot, ending the war as the third-ranking British ace with 60 victories to his credit.

That tributes like this fell into disuse is not surprising. Quite apart from the decline in the sense of chivalry of combatants as compared to that in the First World War, it should be borne in mind that the aircraft in the Second World War, because of their far greater speeds and mostly enclosed cockpits, were not well suited to drop largish objects from.

This was also a factor where delivering messages in general was concerned, as we shall see in the next chapter.

---

* Balbo was a famous man because he had organized and led successful mass formation flights with Savoia-Marchetti S-55s across both the South and North Atlantic, in 1930 and 1933. For a long time afterwards the term 'balbo' was used by English-speaking pilots to denote a large formation of aircraft.

5

Courtesy towards the living

COURTESY is one of the main features of chivalry. It is therefore only natural that in the air war, in which chivalry played a not unimportant part, there should be numerous instances of civilities being exchanged between adversaries. They seldom met in person, however, on the ground. These rare occasions are treated separately, in Chapter 6 of this book. In the air, pilots sometimes waved to their opponents, as Lanoe Hawker did to Manfred von Richthofen during their epic duel, which ended in Hawker's death.*

On 28 November 1915 Lieutenant Grinnell-Milne and his observer (16 Sqn RFC), flying a BE2c, had just shot down a two-seater Albatros west of Lille, when they were attacked by four other German planes. During this engagement they were for some moments flying very close alongside one of the enemy planes.

> Our own gun was momentarily out of action, between mountings,** and we could see the enemy observer working over his as though reloading or clearing a jam. We were actually close enough to see the expression upon each other's faces, but powerless to do harm. I don't know yet what came over me, whether nervousness, excitement, or just a fellow-feeling for the man opposite in the same position as myself; but it was at any rate a joyful impulse that made me raise my

* See previous chapter.

** The BE2c had only one gun, operated by the observer, who occupied the front cockpit. He could place the gun on any one of a number of mountings. While changing from one mounting to another he could, of course, not fire the gun.

arm to wave across the narrow air space. And from the gunner's cockpit of that enemy biplane, the German waved back to me. Just a single wave of the arm above the head, a salute a salute as it might have been in the days of tilting, of knights in armour and of wooden lances — or perhaps as boxers shake hands in the ring. Then, his gun being ready, he opened fire. My observer was still loading, I was forced to turn away in self-protection. Personally I had only an automatic pistol, but I discharged it defiantly. . . .[1]

That gestures could easily be misinterpreted is evident from a description that Albert Ball (then 60 Sqn RFC) gave of a fight he had on 25 September 1916 with a German two-seater, as compared with the actual facts. Flying his favourite Nieuport 17, Ball attacked an Aviatik C-type that was heading for the Allied lines near Bucquoy. It was a plane from *Fliegerabteilung A.237*,* based at Vendhuille, with an experienced crew. They gave a good account of themselves, duelling with the agile little Nieuport for half an hour, an unusually long time for an air combat. It was a losing fight for them, though. Ball ran out of ammunition, but by then the intermittent bursts from his Lewis gun had killed the observer, *Leutnant* Hoffmann, and seriously wounded the pilot, named Tewes. But Ball was completely unaware of this. Describing the fight in a letter home he wrote:

> We kept on firing until we had used up all our ammunition. There was nothing more to be done after that, so we both burst out laughing. We couldn't help it — it was so ridiculous. We flew side by side laughing at each other for a few seconds, and then we waved adieu to each other and went off. He was a real sport that Hun.

Later, in his home town, he said about this fight to a news reporter: "I should have been sorry had I killed him, and I think he would have been sorry too had he finished me off."[2]

With the gesture Tewes made he must have been trying to indicate to Ball the desperate state he and his observer were in; possibly it was a gesture of surrender. As to his laughing, this must have been a grimace of pain.

Ball's kind words about his adversaries in this fight are a bit surprising, as he was not noted for a chivalrous attitude. Willie

---

* The 'A' stood for *Artillerie*. The *Fliegerbteilungen* with artillery co-operation duties were numbered from 200 upwards.

Fry, who knew and flew with Albert Ball, describes him as a "skilled and dedicated killer with no other motive than to use his machine and armament to shoot down enemy aeroplanes. There was in his attitude none of that sporting element which to a certain extent formed the basis of many scout pilots' approach to air fighting."[3]

There were in the First World War more instances of pilots waving to one another after an indecisive combat, before parting and going their several ways home. But apparently it did not happen frequently. There is a story that the American pilot Raoul Lufbery, who was the most brilliant star of the *Escadrille Lafayette*, once waved to his adversary after both he and the German had exhausted their ammunition, and that the German waved back. Parsons writes that Lufbery's opponent was Oswald Boelcke,[4] but this is quite impossible. At the time the encounter is supposed to have taken place (August 1916), Boelcke had not yet returned from his journey to Turkey, and afterwards served in the Somme sector of the front, whereas Lufbery was at Verdun.

Another — more reliable — author tells us that in September or October 1916 Lufbery once broke off a duel with a Fokker because he had seen a smoke signal, fired by a French anti-aircraft battery to indicate that an enemy aircraft was crossing the lines, and it was his first duty to try to intercept it. He waved to his German adversary and dived westward. The pilot of the Fokker returned the salute and, for reasons of his own, did not pursue the American but headed down for his base at Habsheim.[5]

Examples of pilots saluting each other during or after combat in the Second World War are much harder to find. In one case, on 3 May 1940, a Lockheed Hudson of RAF Coastal Command was attacked near Borkum by three Messerschmitt Bf 109s. The rear gunner shot one of them down, but was killed almost immediately afterwards. This made the Hudson practically defenceless against the two other Germans, who kept firing at it, without succeeding in bringing it down, however. When they had run out of ammunition, the Messerschmitt pilots pulled alongside the Hudson, waved to the pilot and waggled their wings in appreciation of the valour of the crew before turning back. The pilot and the navigator of the

101

Hudson were both wounded, but managed to bring their riddled aircraft home.[6]

In some other cases it is not clear whether the situation was indeed such that neither side was able to continue fighting, or that it was a case of one pilot being so chivalrous that he did not choose to kill a defenceless enemy, and indicated this by waving his hand or by simply breaking away.

Civilities of far more importance and interest were contained in the many messages that were dispatched back and forth between the belligerents, especially in the First World War. They ranged from serious communications, asking or giving information regarding missing men, to jesting remarks.

Under the Geneva Convention the belligerents are required to notify each other of all captures of prisoners. If they are wounded or sick, this should be mentioned. Also the names of those who were killed in action or died in captivity should be communicated. The Convention prescribes that all this should be done as soon as possible. However, communications through the official channels were not very fast. The air forces had a quicker way; they could drop messages on the airfields of the enemy, or — if that appeared too dangerous — anywhere else in enemy territory where they were sure to be found. This method had the added advantage that one was not restricted to words. All kinds of things could be included with the message: photographs, personal effects, identity discs, or whatever, even a wreath, as we have seen in the preceding chapter.

The first time such a message was delivered by air appears to have been on 11 September 1914, when a German aeroplane dropped a note in the French lines telling of the capture of one of their pilots.[7] It has been noted that "it is not clear whether this was the same case as that mentioned by M. Mortane in *La Guerre aérienne,* 7 November 1918, p.835, where he states that when Lieut. Faurit was captured in Châlons Camp in September 1914 a German aircraft dropped a message to say that he was a prisoner and in good health."[8]

The practice of dropping messages had become common by the spring of 1915. In the *Daily Mail* of 3 May 1915 a Mr. Beach Thomas reported that

> on several occasions of late German airmen have dropped letters giving news — in some cases delivering autograph

letters — of British prisoners in Germany. In every instance
our airmen have flown over the German lines to drop a letter
of thanks and acknowledgement.

From countless sources we know that the practice was
generally observed throughout the First World War and on
every front. The Australian official historian's statement about
this may be quoted as typical: "This method of correspondence
between opposing airmen was a feature of war in the air on all
fronts."[9]

Of course there were exceptions. Sometimes a certain sector
of the front seems to have had a bad name with respect to
chivalry:

> A Fee [FE2c; of 100 Sqn RAF] crashed [on 17 May, 1918], and
> with a gesture of chivalry rare in this sector [Metz] a German
> aeroplane dropped a message across the Lines to say that 2nd
> Lieut J. C. Williamson and Lieut N. F. Penruddocke were
> unhurt."[10]

And then there were always those whose hatred for the
enemy was for some reason so great that there was in their
hearts no room for any noble feelings towards him. Such a man
was the French ace René Dorme, who flew with Georges
Guynemer in the famous *Escadrille 3* of the *Cigognes* Group.
Dorme was a native of Lorraine, and in addition to the Stork
insignia he had the Cross of Lorraine painted on his aircraft.
Also he carried with him, by way of a mascot, a little doll in
Alsatian dress. The freeing of Alsace-Lorraine from German
occupation clearly was the cause he was fighting for with such
bitterness. When, in March 1917, a German he had brought
down handed him a letter in which he informed his parents that
he was only wounded, and asked Dorme to drop it across the
lines, the Frenchman did take the letter but intentionally kept
it with him, "as a souvenir". "He may be damned, and his
parents may remain without news. French parents suffer
enough through them," Dorme wrote in a letter.[11]

Such a low attitude was most unusual, however. Happily,
there were many more cases in which a fine sense of honour
governed the behaviour of airmen towards their captives. The
following incidents show that occasionally far more was done
than was required or could be expected.

On 8 July 1917 Lieutenant C. H. Vautin of the Australian

Flying Corps was driven down near Gaza (Palestine) and captured. Another AFC officer, Captain C. A. Brooks, was killed in the same combat. Two days later, *Leutnant* Gerhard Felmy of the German Air Service sent a message by aeroplane to say that Brooks had been killed and buried with military honours, and that Vautin was quite well and hoped his kit would be sent to him. Letters from Vautin and photographs of Vautin and Felmy, taken together, were enclosed in the bag that was dropped. On receipt of this message, Captain Murray Jones of the AFC flew to the German aerodrome at Huj with Vautin's kit and letters from home, and dropped them from a height of 50 feet. He was in no way molested by the Germans, who, indeed, waved to him, a salutation which he returned. "The incident," says the official historian, "affords a pleasing picture of the knightly fashion in which airmen frequently treated each other between determined duels."[12]

In his book *The Way of the Eagle* Captain Charles J. Biddle, the flying lawyer,* and from June 1918 the commander of the 13th Aero Squadron of the American Air Service, describes how on 16 August 1918 he forced down a Rumpler two-seater, which victory was his fifth and made him an ace. He had killed the observer and wounded the pilot, who then landed his slightly damaged plane behind the French lines at Nancy. Biddle writes: "I have got a little parachute to which I am attaching a note giving the names of the men and a short statement of what happened to them, and this I shall drop over the German lines the first clear day. . . . The Hun aviation in this sector is very good about doing the same thing and sending us information about any of our men who are lost, so the least we can do is to reciprocate."[13]

The German ace *Hauptmann* Adolf Ritter von Tutschek, who wore the *Pour le Mérite*, tells how he went to see the crew of a British two-seater he had shot down:

> On the way back I visited the two Englishmen, who were both still alive. Had a long talk with the Flight leader, a really splendid young English captain, shot in the throat and body.

* Charles Biddle was a graduate of Princeton University and Harvard Law School, was admitted to the bar in 1914 and practised law until the spring of 1917, when he joined the French Air Service. After the war he had a highly successful law practice in Philadelphia.

He made me promise to visit him in England after the war, and was very grateful when I undertook to throw a card in his own writing, for his mother, over the English lines. Unfortunately he died of his wounds a fortnight after. [. . .] It was a strange coincidence that I said to the English captain in jest, to console him, that if I should be wounded I should come to the same hospital and keep him company. That very evening I lay beside him, shot through the shoulder![14]

On 20 March 1917 a two-seater of the Austro-Hungarian *Luftfahrttruppen* was brought down in the Italian lines by Luigi Olivari. One of the Austrians, *Leutnant* d'Heintochl, was killed. The next evening an Austrian plane dropped a note addressed to d'Heintochl by his wife, who believed he was alive and a prisoner. An Italian airman dropped a reply, informing her that her husband had died a gallant death and had been buried with military honours.[15]

When 2nd Lieutenant F. N. Grimwade, RFC, was shot down in the German lines on 4 April 1916 the following message was dropped from a German aeroplane in the British lines:

4.4.16. To the Royal Flying Corps, Bailleul. Mr. Grimwade and Mr. Frost have fallen wounded into honourable imprisonment. Mr. Frost has a fleshwound in the thigh, Mr. Grimwade a wound in the thighbone (both bullet wounds). Under the circumstances both are doing well and wish to be remembered to their comrades and relatives.[16]

In March 1916 a German observation plane operating on the Russian front got engine trouble, was then hit by anti-aircraft fire, and had to land in enemy territory. A few days later the Germans were informed by 'air mail' that both the observer, *Leutnant* Lehmann, and his pilot, *Offizierstellvertreter* Thiele, had come down alive and unhurt. On three days in succession the Russians dropped this news. The first time it was playfully written on a 45-feet-long strip of paper. The next day a letter from *Leutnant* Lehmann himself was delivered. The third time the information was given in a letter from the Russian pilots, in which they also teased the Germans by adding that they expected more of them. The Germans took this in good part: "This sportsmanlike-fraternal feeling between pilots is wonderful." In return they dropped the information that the news had been received, with their thanks.[17]

Besides matter-of-fact information about the airmen who had been killed or taken prisoner, the messages on occasion contained words of admiration and praise for the way they had fought, in phrases like "He fought bravely and well", "He died a gallant death" and "He fell after a heroic fight".

It is rather surprising to find that in the First World War — a time when photography was not yet as common as it is today — photographs were often enclosed with the messages. Usually they were photographs of the funeral or the grave of the man whose death was reported.

When the French ace *Capitaine* René Doumer, the commander of *Escadrille SPA.88*, was killed in air combat on 26 April 1917 the French received a message telling of his fate, with two photographs of his grave, one being intended for his wife.[18]

Captain Wedgwood Benn reports that when a British two-seater was brought down near Levico, on the Italian front, the Austrian airmen dropped a note in which they said: "These two officers met their death in aerial combat and are buried in our cemetery of heroes at Levico." Two photographs were enclosed, one showing the funeral procession headed by a priest in robes carrying a crucifix, the other the coffin being lowered into the grave with some of the leading Austrian flying men paraded to do it honour.[19]

A British flying officer writes that the Germans

> used to come over our lines to drop particulars of our missing airmen, letting us know whether they were dead, wounded, or prisoners, and in many cases going to a lot of trouble and into those details which made just all the difference to those suffering at home. My brother, who transferred from the Deccan Horse, and his companion, Lieut. Gordon Smith, were shot down over Bruges in 1915, and not only did the Germans soon after drop full particulars, including the location of the grave, but they also sent later a photograph of the spot, showing a tombstone ingeniously made from parts of the damaged machine.[20]

Another case in point is the delivery of a photograph of Manfred von Richthofen's funeral to the Germans, in April 1918.*

* See page 74

Sometimes a less melancholy photograph was received, of someone who had been taken prisoner. There might be a snapshot of him, together with the man who had brought him down, or among a group of adversaries entertaining him. Those who sent off the messages were often so courteous as to write them in the enemy's language. This made for some unusual phraseology now and then. But this seldom, if ever, detracted from the intelligibility of the message, and at times lent it an endearing charm. One can visualize the smiles on the lips of the Australian airmen when they received a letter from the German *Leutnant* Felmy, beginning "All dear sports".[21]

The following letter was sent to the RFC by the Germans on the Salonika front, when Lieutenant S. J. M. White and H. Matthews had been killed in an air combat in January 1917:

> THE ROYAL FLYING CORPS. — The German aviators are very sorry to inform you of the death of the two English aviators which were killed on the 15th January, 10.30 A.M., after a fight with our aeroplanes. The English aviators had been fighting very bravely, but their aeroplane dropped after about five minutes fight and "skilled". They died as heroes, and have all our respects. Their bodies will be buried with all military honours.
>
> We are informing you also of your Lieut. Pocock having been made a prisoner by the troops without being blessed.
>
> We are obliged of your having informed us of the four German aviators which have been made your prisoners.
>
> "THE GERMAN FLYING CORPS."[22]

It is not quite clear what was meant by "skilled", probably "crashed" or something like that. Apparently unsure whether it was the correct word, the Germans put inverted commas round it. In the second paragraph the word "blessed" is used for "wounded", with the French word *blessé* in mind.

It occasionally happened that with a message items were dropped for a comrade who had been taken prisoner. Things a man would need or like to have in captivity: clothes (a uniform sometimes), identity papers he had not with him when captured, letters from home, money, cigarettes, chocolate, etc.

On 18 August 1917 Sergeant Harold B. Willis was one of six American fighter pilots of the *Escadrille Lafayette* who escorted 31 Sopwith 1½ Strutters of the French *Groupe de Bombardement I*, which were to raid Dun-sur-Meuse, a vital railway centre north of Verdun. Shortly before reaching the target the formation was attacked by Albatros fighters. In a duel with one of them, Willis's SPAD was so badly damaged that he had to land in enemy territory. One of the Germans flew over him, waved his hand, turned and landed nearby — followed by two others. "They all saluted very properly as they came up — young chaps, perfectly correct." Less than an hour later Willis was sitting at a mess table having breakfast with the Germans, before being driven away to the prison-fortress at Montmédy. As it was a hot day, Willis had taken off that morning wearing only his pyjamas and an old greasy brown sweater under his flying suit; he carried no identification, no cigarettes and no money. Alone in his cell, a prisoner in Germany, Willis sat down on his cot "and cried like a baby".[23]

Harold's squadron mates had seen him go down, but did not know what his fate had been. Later that day Edwin Parsons, one of his best friends, "fixed up a message, put it in a cardboard cylinder, hung it on a little silk parachute and dropped it far in the German lines, asking for news. Two days later an artillery outfit away up the lines telephoned that they had an answer. Willy was a prisoner, but in good health. So I wrapped his uniform, boots, cigarettes and money in a nice package and took them over, being careful to address the bundle to *Leutnant* Harold Willis."[24] He falsified Willis's rank because officers got better treatment in a POW camp than non-coms did. He was confident that Willis would have been smart enough to claim commissioned rank, there being no uniform or identity papers to give him the lie. To be sure, it was not a very gentlemanlike thing to do. Willis made several abortive attempts to escape from captivity before, towards the end of the war, he at last succeeded in breaking out of the prison camp at Villengen in Baden. He reached France just in time for taking part in the Armistice celebrations.

Naturally, flying over enemy territory to deliver a friendly message could be as dangerous as going there with hostile intentions, especially if one overflew an enemy aerodrome. To ensure that those for whom the message was intended would get it, and get it quickly, one ran risks, as is illustrated by an incident in the Middle East theatre of war. On 8 March 1917 a Fokker flew over El Arish aerodrome, then in British hands, and dropped two letters from British airmen who had been captured a few days before and one addressed to a German prisoner. The Fokker was attacked by mistake. But in true chivalrous fashion the British squadron sent two planes to Beersheba (in Turkish hands) to thank the Germans for the trouble they had taken and to apologize for the attack on the message-carrier.[25] One cannot help speculating what would have happened if the Fokker had been forced down, and would like to think that if the plane were not irreparable and the pilot still able to fly, he would have been given the opportunity to take off again and regain his base, although the incident would then almost certainly have been carefully omitted from any official report! But one can hardly quarrel with anyone who thinks that such generous behaviour would strain the idea of sportsmanship to quite unrealistic lengths.[26]

In view of the risks attending the delivery of such "air mail"* messages to the enemy, it is remarkable that the method was also used for non-essential communications with the enemy, for example to wish him a Happy Easter or a Merry Christmas and a Happy New Year. On Easter Sunday, 1915, for instance, the Russians dropped an enormous Easter egg, with the inscription "Christ is risen", from an aeroplane. It was attached to a parachute and came down slowly on the Austrian lines.[27]

There were more such courtesies.

> The messages exchanged before the first fall of Przemysl between the Russian and Austrian air forces were particularly courteous and friendly, almost (one would think) to the point of indiscretion, and this at a time (early in 1915) when feeling was otherwise bitter on the Russo-Austrian front.[28]

J.M. Spaight in his *Air Power and War Rights* quotes numerous "friendly-foemanly" messages to prove his point, providing further evidence that there was a very special rapport between the flyers on both sides, in contrast with the feelings the ground troops had for the enemy.

We are indebted to *Oberleutnant* Schütz for a number of anecdotes illustrating the friendly communion there was

---

* The terms *Poste aérienne militaire* and *Kriegsluftpost* were actually used at the time. See the reproduction of a Russian message, in both French and German, to Austro-Hungarian flyers in May 1917, in: Ernst Peter, *Die k.u.k. Luftschiffer- und Fliegertruppe Österreich-Ungarns 1794-1919* (1981), p.179.

between the air forces opposing one another in the Middle East.[29]

One day, he writes, the British pilots even invited the Germans to come and have a cup of tea with them on a "neutral" landing-ground. The Germans thought best not to accept the invitation, however. They did not suspect foul play, but simply thought that such fraternization would go too far.

In April 1917, when Schütz returned to Iraq from Germany, where he had fetched some new aeroplanes, the British dropped the following message:

> The British airmen send their compliments to Captain S. and are pleased to welcome him back to Mesopotamia. We shall be pleased to offer him a warm reception in the air. We enclose a tin of English cigarettes, and will send him a Baghdad melon when they are in season. *Au revoir*. Our compliments to the other German airmen. The Royal Flying Corps.

The main motive of the British for sending the note may have been to tease the Germans by demonstrating how well informed they were about the comings and goings of enemy personnel. If so, it was a gentle way of teasing, as was also the case when they dropped a sack containing some rusty old spare parts for an aeroplane which the Germans, unable to get replacements from Germany, had "home-built" in Mesopotamia. Attached to it was a label "With the compliments of the Royal Air Force".

Lieutenant-Colonel Tennant, who was serving in the RFC in Mesopotamia at the time, describes Schütz as "a fine fighter and a gentleman".

> Sometimes he would drop a note on the aerodrome; he asked us to send over the *Sketch* and the *Bystander*, and stated that they were tired of the records captured with a gramophone at Kut, would we send them some new ones, especially 'Tipperary'; in return for this they would drop us fresh vegetables from Baghdad.[30]

The play element is very pronounced in these last cases. Many more similar cases are on record, but one has to be wary of accepting every one of them as genuine. Rather too often writers have failed to resist the temptation to embellish the stories connected with such messages, or have even made them up.

There is, for instance, the tale of the American pilot Bert Hall and the fur gloves. According to this story, it happened early in the First World War that a German pilot lost an expensive fur glove while flying over a French aerodrome. Hall, who was stationed there, picked it up. The following day the German came back and dropped the other glove with a note in which he begged the finder to accept it with his compliments, as he had no use for one of a pair. Hall was delighted to accept the gift and dropped a note in return, with his sincere thanks to the donor.[31]

The very fact that Hall himself must have told this story, or at least contributed to it, makes it highly suspect. Weston Bert Hall*, who served in the *Escadrille Lafayette* for about six months, was a genial and charming man, adventure personified, but absolutely untrustworthy. He told fantastic lies. Nobody could even be certain that Hall was his real name. Some of his fantasies nearly involved the *Escadrille's* name with that of Mata Hari, the notorious spy. He cheated at cards, forged cheques, and made false claims to having shot down enemy aircraft. One pilot wrote to a friend in Paris: "As we all know, Hall is an awful liar and hot-air artist who rushes in to report a victory every time he sees something burning on the ground." All this resulted in the other pilots forcing him to leave the *Escadrille* at the end of 1916. He went to another French unit, from which he deserted to America. Much later, in 1932, he was sentenced to two and a half years imprisonment, for swindle.[32] In short, a most disreputable fellow!

I have included the story of the gloves not so much because it is an agreeable one in the context of this chapter, but because it just might be true and is certainly not inconsistent with the attitude of the airmen towards their enemies in those times, which I want to illustrate.

The play element does not necessarily include humour. However, unless a message concerned the death of a combatant, humour was seldom lacking in the communication that was carried on between airmen of opposing sides. The humour could be quite inoffensive, but was often facetious. Occasionally it was not immediately apparent, as when the Germans weighted a packet of messages with bits of coal, "to show them

* Not to be confused with his compatriot and contemporary, James Norman Hall!

111

over there that we are still far removed from a scarcity of coal".[33]

Needless to say, the recipient of a teasing message was not always in the right mood to appreciate its humour. Colonel Billy Mitchell, chief of the US Air Service, 1st Corps, certainly was not when in July 1918 he received a facetious message from the Germans to the effect that they had captured an entire US squadron intact, the only American bombing squadron, too.

In the early evening of 10 July 1918 six Breguet 14B-2 two-seater bombers of the 96th Aero Squadron took off from their aerodrome near Gondrecourt for a daylight raid against enemy railway yards at Conflans. Major Harry M. Brown, the squadron commander, led the formation. The weather proved worse than they had expected and they were soon flying without any visual contact with the ground. After an hour or so, Major Brown signalled the others that he was lost. Their situation was even worse than he thought. Since they had taken off, a strong south-west wind had sprung up, which had driven them far into Germany. With their fuel running low, they carefully descended through the clouds. All six pilots managed to land safely. They came down near a large city which, to their astonishment and dismay, turned out to be the German town of Koblenz, on the confluence of the Moselle and the Rhine, more than a hundred miles from their intended target! The Germans captured the 12 crew members and all the planes fell into their hands intact. No lives were lost, but it was a terrible blow to the US Air Service. The 96th Aero had begun operations less than a month before and now had only one plane left and very few flying officers. Within hours the US Air Service headquarters received the following message from the Germans: "We thank you for the fine airplanes and equipment which you sent us, but what will we do with the Major?" Mitchell flew into a rage. In his diary he wrote:

> This was the worst exhibition of worthlessness that we ever had on the front . . . needless to say we did not reply about the major as he was better off in Germany at that time than he would have been with us.[34]

In the Second World War there were few instances of airmen dispatching — unofficial — messages to their adversaries.

112

Indeed, compared with what was done in the First World War, their number may be considered negligible, especially if one takes into account that so many more aircraft and airmen were involved in the later war.

This can be partly explained by the unmistakable fact that there was less chivalry in the Second World War than in the First. But there were other factors as well, of a technical nature. The greater speed of the aircraft and their enclosed cockpits made it very difficult for the pilot or another crew member to drop a small packet with any accuracy on an airfield or other place where it was sure to be found. Also, it had to be done from a low height, and such places would be well protected by anti-aircraft defences, which were much more effective than those of 25 years before. Moreover, the official channels through which the belligerents could get into contact with each other if necessary were much better in the Second World War. This removed one important motive for taking more or less unofficial action by dropping messages to the enemy, namely the wish to get (and give) news about airmen who had not returned to their bases in a quicker way than through official channels.

In the Second World War the sending of messages to the enemy — by dropping them on his territory or otherwise — had become so unusual, that J. M. Spaight calls them "echoes of the First World War"[35]. One of the instances he gives is that of Flying Officer E. M. ("Imshi") Mason of 274 Sqn RAF, top scorer of the First Lybian Campaign, who in February 1941 flew in his Hurricane to an Italian aerodrome near Benghazi, to drop a letter from a captured Italian pilot to his mother.

Another case Spaight cites is unlike the others in that the message did not have to be delivered across the lines; it was from a German prisoner-of-war in England to the RAF pilot who had brought him down, during the Battle of Britain. In the morning of 27 September 1940 a Junkers Ju 88 A-1 of *Aufklärungsgruppe 123* was on a photo-reconnaissance mission to Liverpool when it was attacked over North Devon by Pilot Officer E. S. Marss of 152 Sqn in a Spitfire. The Junkers had to ditch in the sea at Porlock Bay, Somerset. One of the crew was dead; the three others were made prisoners. A few days later the Spitfire pilot received this note through a brother officer:

"The pilot of the German plane Ju 88* shot down this morning by P/O Marss sends him a message of congratulations on a very fine fight. He would like to meet him."[36]

The scene of the next two examples is north-west Abyssinia, towards the end of the British campaign that liberated that country from the Italians.

In the late afternoon of 24 October 1941 South African pilots of 3 Sqn SAAF at Dabat heard what was probably an enemy aircraft flying southwards in the direction of Lake Tana. At first they could not see it because of the low, heavy clouds, but moments later they glimpsed a Fiat CR 42 fighter through a gap in the clouds. Two of the pilots took off in pursuit, in their Gloster Gladiators. One of them, unable to find the Italian, soon returned, but the other, Lieutenant Hope, sighted the Fiat and pursued it until he caught up with it over Ambazzo. He dived on the Italian and opened fire. There followed a short duel — between two obsolescent biplanes, truly an echo of the former war! — a duel that was won by Hope. The Fiat caught fire and spun into the ground. In the words of the official historian:

> Lt. Hope circled the funeral pyre of the last Italian airman to be killed in combat in the Abyssinian campaign. The fight had lasted barely two minutes and had ended almost symbolically, as the sun set among the great cold peaks.[37]

The next day a South African ground party sent from Dabat found the wreck of the Fiat just off the Gondar road, the charred body of the pilot still in the cockpit. The South African pilots were touched by the death of this lone pilot. A farewell tribute was dropped on Ambazzo by Lieutenant Hope.[38] Colonel Dario Busoni of the *Regia Aeronautica* in Gondar radioed the text of this message to Rome: "Tribute to pilot of Fiat. He was a brave one. — South African Air Force."[39]

A week after his victory Lieutenant Hope was himself shot down. After dark on 31 October he took off in a Gloster Gladiator, planning to attack an Italian ground convoy on the mountain road from Gorgora, on Lake Tana, to Gondar. The jetties at Gorgora, where motor-boats brought in supplies,

---

* He was *Oberleutnant* Willi Rude. Eric Marss was killed in action on 24 July 1941 over Brest, from where Willi Rude had taken off for his reconnaissance flight to Liverpool ten months before.

had already been attacked several times, but Hope made the dangerous night flight on his own initiative, without authorization. It seems he was a great believer in astrology and had found the position of the stars and planets favourable for his venture. He did indeed find a transport column, but when he attacked it with his four machine-guns he was hit by the Italian return fire and his plane burst into flames. He had to crash-land in the darkness at 200 mph. Although his face was severely burnt, he miraculously survived the crash and also some rough treatment at the hands of an excited askari, who shot him in the head and whacked him with a rifle butt before he was rescued by two Italian officers. Lieutenant Hope's comrades, who had learned of his fate from a Rome Radio announcement, did not know all those details until ten days later, when a man of the Habash tribe — often used as messengers by the Italians — brought in a letter from Hope which he had written in hospital. In it he asked for cigarettes, shaving kit, toothbrush and an Italian-English dictionary. "In the exchange of civilized courtesies which followed, toilet articles were dropped by a home-made parachute on Azozo, Gondar's airfield."[40]

Though rare, light-hearted messages were not unknown in the Second World War, as is witnessed by the following two cases.

In a German raid on an airfield in Malta, in 1942, one of the attacking bombers was hit and so badly damaged that the crew had to bale out. They landed safely. This must have been observed by other German airmen, for later that same day, during a second raid on the same aerodrome, a steel canister was dropped. It was found lying on the ground with an inscription on it — "To the Air Officer Commanding, Malta: On our word of honour this does not contain explosives of any kind." Even so, it was approached with great caution and only opened under the direction of bomb-disposal experts. Inside there was a letter, also addressed to the Air Officer Commanding, Malta, reading:

> SIR,
> Re Hans von —— who was shot down over this aerodrome this morning, will you please set him to write out twenty-five times 'I must carry my identity disc when flying!'

115

In the canister were found the airman's identity disc and his razor, shaving brush, toothbrush, toothpaste and other necessaries. Mr. Leslie Oliver, who has recorded the incident, refers to it as "a refreshing, if isolated, deviation from the sordid record of brutal and inhuman attacks which characterised the Germans in their offensive against Malta".[41]

There were few pilots in the air war whose names were generally known to their adversaries. Unless their names — and exploits — could be used to buttress morale, or for propaganda purposes, the censor suppressed them, because they might be of value to the enemy intelligence service, especially if connected with the units the pilots served with.[42]

Heinz-Wolfgang Schnaufer was one of the handful of German pilots in the Second World War who won wartime renown in Britain, as one of the most successful night fighter pilots who defended their country against the devastating attacks by RAF bombers. In fact, he ended the war as the top-scoring night fighter ace of the Second World War, or any war. He scored his first kill on 2 June 1942 when he was not yet 20 years of age, and never looked back. Fighting with tireless energy, aggressively, at times like a man obsessed, Schnaufer accumulated victory upon victory. Several times he scored more than one in a night, on one occasion no fewer than seven! His final tally was 121, and with good reason one can say that this achievement ranks him second to none among the fighter aces, night or day. As a general rule it was much more difficult to win a night victory than to shoot down an enemy aircraft by day, and it is not at all far-fetched to put Schnaufer's score on a par with the highest victory score of all time, that of Erich Hartmann: 352 day victories.

The RAF bomber crews knew about Schnaufer, feared him, but also admired him. "His name and tales of his wild assaults on the Lancasters and Halifaxes were discussed in many an RAF mess."[43] The British nicknamed Schnaufer "The Night Ghost of St. Trond", after St. Trond (Flemish: St. Truiden) in Belgium, his operational base. On Major Schnaufer's 23rd birthday a military radio station at Calais actually broadcast a birthday greeting to him, in which they told him that they respected him for the fair way in which he fought. In his honour they played a BBC dance orchestra recording of *The Night Ghost*.[44]

116

Heinz-Wolfgang Schnaufer survived the war, for the last six months of which he had been *Kommodore* of *NJG (Nachtjagd-geschwader) -4*, wearing Germany's highest decoration, the Knight's Cross with Oak Leaves and Swords with Diamonds.[45] His aircraft, a night fighter version of the Messerschmitt Bf 110, which type he had flown in combat almost exclusively, was for some time exhibited in Hyde Park in London. Part of its tail, with the 121 victory marks painted on it, is still on display in the Imperial War Museum.

In 1950 Schnaufer was killed in a road accident in France.

Messages to the enemy could sometimes contain a challenge to fight. We have already seen something of the kind in the British message to *Oberleutnant* Schütz in April 1917: "We shall be pleased to offer him a warm reception in the air."* Challenging an adversary to fight, especially to a duel, is traditionally associated with chivalry. Again, the play element is evident.

An early example of a challenge in the air war is the following message to Max Immelmann, six copies of which were dropped by 13 Sqn RFC on 13 November 1915.

> A British officer-pilot is anxious to meet the redoubtable Capt. Immelmann in fair fight. The suggested rendezvous is a point above the first line trenches just east of Hebuterne. The British officer will be there from 10 a.m.-11 a.m. daily from November 15 till November 30 weather permitting. It is to be understood that only one aeroplane can be sent to meet this challenge, and that no anti-aircraft gun may fire at either combatant.[46]

Although 13 Sqn dropped the messages, it was 11 Sqn that was to provide officers to be at the rendezvous daily, presumably taking turns, which would explain why the British officer was not mentioned by name, rather unusual in a challenge. Nothing came of it, however. It is not even clear if Immelmann ever got to know of the challenge, though there seems to be evidence that the message was received by the Germans.

Quite a few legends have been woven round Jean Navarre, one of the early French aces, a daring and romantic young man, who used to fly with a lady's silk stocking on his head, instead of a flying helmet. One fantastic story has it that when,

* See page 109.

117

in the night of 21/22 March 1915, several aeroplanes of *Escadrille M.S. 12* took off to intercept Zeppelins which were — mistakenly — reported over Paris, Navarre carried a kitchen knife, hoping to come close enough to a Zepplin to be able to slash the monster with it![47] More plausible — and altogether in keeping with Navarre's character, too — is the story that he once challenged Oswald Boelcke to a duel. But before the day arrived which he had named, Navarre was wounded, and an inexperienced fellow pilot, Pérouse, took his place. Boelcke did not appear at the rendezvous, which undoubtedly saved Pérouse's life.[48]

There was no lack of colourful characters in the French Flying Service in the First World War. Charles Nungesser was another one. Like Navarre, he had learned to fly before the war. After some adventurous years in South America, he returned to France just before the war. He first joined a cavalry regiment, but transferred to the *Aviation Militaire* in January 1915. He was a notorious womanizer, and is rumoured to have been one of Mata Hari's many lovers. Lieutenant Nungesser ended the war with 45 victories to his credit. They had not been easily come by: he was wounded no fewer than 17 times, in air combat and in crashes, and spent a lot of time in hospital. In the middle of May 1917 Nungesser was shown a note that had been dropped from a German aeroplane, inviting him that day to single combat over Douai. He promptly took off to accept the challenge. At the rendezvous not one, but six enemy fighters waited for him. A dogfight followed, during which Nungesser shot down two of the Germans in flames, *Leutnant* Schweizer and *Gefreiter* Bittorf.[49] A proper retribution for a dishonourable deed.

An idiosyncrasy of Nungesser's was that he had macabre emblems painted on all the aeroplanes he flew in. At first it was only a skull and crossbones. Later a coffin flanked by two lighted funeral candles was added, all these — for some obscure reason — within a heart-shaped outline. These markings were also carried on the Levasseur PL-8 *L'Oiseau Blanc*, the aircraft in which Nungesser and François Coli, his navigator, took off from Le Bourget aerodrome, north of Paris, on 8 May 1927, in an attempt to fly nonstop to New York. They disappeared without a trace. Two weeks later Charles Lindbergh touched down at Le Bourget after his

Charles Nungesser's Nieuport 27 with his personal macabre insignia.

(IWM)

successful New York-Paris flight.

Challenging adversaries to fight was not unknown in the Second World War, either. In his autobiography Colin Hodgkinson* tells of an incident in June 1943 which, he says,

> might be unique in the war. Some of us heard a voice on the R/T addressing our C.O. 'We're going to get you, Charles,' it growled dramatically, in effect. 'You've lived too long. We know what you look like and we've got you on our list.' There followed a challenge from a German *Staffel*, based apparently at Caen, to meet 611 [Sqn] at 20,000 over the Channel on a day to be decided by mutual radio-telephony exchanges. We all took a good view of this exciting prospect which harked back to the brave days when champions jousted for their respective sides. Our 'Y' service** confirmed the message and Jack Charles, very much in favour, sent his formal acceptance. But Fighter Command smelt a German ambush and, to our great disappointment, nothing came of this laudable effort to inject a little medieval spirit into a too mechanical war.[50]

As a matter of fact, this challenge by radio to 611 Sqn RAF

---

* See note 34 to chapter 6.
** The service whose task it was to listen in to the enemy's radio messages.

was not unique in the 1939-1945 war. Similar cases have been reported from the Russian front. In 1943 the Soviet Air Force had begun concentrating their best pilots in the élite Red Guard units. Günther Rall, the third-ranking German ace, with 275 victories, describes these Russian pilots as "the real fighter types — individualists — not the dull masses of the ordinary squadrons". They would often tune their radio transmissions to German wavelengths, challenging the Luftwaffe's best aces to come up and fight.[51]

These challenges, exemplifying the growing self-confidence of the Soviet airmen which I mentioned at the end of chapter 2, almost certainly were not challenges in the true chivalric tradition, daring an adversary to fight an honourable duel, or a group of adversaries to a contest between equal numbers. But then, very few challenges in the air war really were that, even in the First World War.

The instances I have given do illustrate the playful character that modern warfare still retained in some small measure, in spite of being as a whole inhuman, but they can hardly serve to support our findings that chivalry definitely played a part in the air war. Especially not because, as far as I know, there is no reliable report of an honourable challenge having been taken up in the same spirit and resulting in a chivalrous fight. This fact need not surprise or disappoint us, though. Medieval history abounds in examples of ceremonial offers of time and place for a battle, but it was the rule to decline or disregard such an offer. The custom was of a purely formal nature.[52]

I will not close this chapter without devoting some space to a very special kind of "messages" to the enemy, contained in words or pictures painted on an aircraft and meant to be seen by an adversary coming near, from behind.

For the most part such phrases or pictures were of an inoffensive nature, at worst somewhat mocking.* At one time Ernst Udet had *Du doch nicht!!* (You won't get me!!) painted on the tail of his Fokker D VII. "Pride goes before a fall," he later wrote about this. The very next day he had been shot down in that aircraft, fortunately being able to save his life with the parachute he was wearing.[53]

* An exception was the word *Schweinhund*, which Capt. Grinnell-Milne displayed on his SE5a fighter.

Although *Leutnant* Fritz Kempf of *Jasta Boelcke* was not one of the better-known pilots in that illustrious *Staffel*, he flaunted his surname on the top wing of his Fokker Dr I triplane, in large, white capital letters on the dark olive green background of the plane. Below that, on the middle wing, an attacker from behind could read: *kennscht mi noch*? (remember me?).[54]

A fine example of an expressive picture was to be seen on the tail-fin of a De Havilland DH4 of 202 Sqn RAF in 1918: the silhouette of a man cocking a snook at anyone coming up from behind.[55]

Anyone who has looked into collections of pictures of operational military aircraft will have been struck by the seemingly endless variety of symbols, mottos, badges, names, pictures (ranging from religious to erotic) and geometrical designs with which aircraft going to war have been decorated, apart from the official national insignia of course. It would be an interesting project to classify these special markings and study them from both a historical and psychological point of view, but this is beyond the scope of the present book. There are, however, some categories of markings which have definite associations with chivalry. As these have nothing much to do with the subject of this chapter, I will deal with them separately, in chapter 7.

6

Friendly encounters with the enemy

AS we have seen, there is between the airmen of the world a definite affinity. It is stronger than that which exists between people of practically every other occupation.

That this was so at the beginnings of aviation is not hard to understand. A small number of adventurous and intrepid men were for the first time leaving the earth and flying like birds, as man had longed to be able to do from the earliest of times. It was only natural that those pioneers, sharing the new and wonderful skills and experiences, the adulation of the public and also the tremendous risks, felt united in what has been variously described as an international brotherhood, a fraternity, a freemasonry of the air.

It is less easy to realize why that bond should have remained in existence later on, when flying became more and more ordinary and safe, and the number of those who could fly an aircraft grew into many tens of thousands. I think the explanation is at once simple and remarkable: the job of flying an aircraft, however commonplace it became, never really lost its enchantment, its very special status. This is not only true with respect to the modern fighter pilot, who — as everyone knows — still has a most exciting and highly dangerous job, flying at fantastic speeds and heights. It also goes for your ordinary airline pilot. He may tell you that he is little more than a glorified taxi-driver. But in his heart of hearts he will know that he is being dishonest. He could tell you that to him, and every other pilot, leaving the earth never ceases to lose its wonder and excitement. That even during an ordinary take-off from an excellent runway, in perfect weather, his pulse-rate nearly doubles. He could tell you that up there, looking down upon the earth, he is seldom completely free from feeling high and mighty.

In other words, being a pilot has certainly not become a dull occupation, but has retained much of the strong appeal it had in the beginning, because of the extraordinary characteristics that distinguish it from every other activity, with the exception nowadays of being an astronaut. And — as in the case of the aviation pioneers — the awareness of doing something exceptional, together with a group of others who have the same interests and feelings, and who know what it is all about, is seminal to the notion of belonging to a world-wide fraternity, however vaguely visualized. This 'membership' is greatly valued; the loss of it is a painful experience. To a true pilot, few worse things can happen than losing his status of actively flying pilot, for medical or other reasons, especially if his work continues to bring him into contact with pilots still flying. "Being a grounded pilot in the midst of flying pilots is torture."[1]

In times of peace there is no lack of opportunities for pilots to meet their *confrères* from other countries. Their very mobility facilitates international contacts.

In wartime, however, the barriers of enmity made normal contacts between airmen on different sides of the conflict impossible. As a matter of fact, the only chance a pilot had of meeting an adversary and having a conversation with him, was in the situation that one or the other was a prisoner-of-war, or had come down in enemy territory and was about to become one. The history of the First World War in the air abounds in stories of such contacts, and, knowing of the 'comradeship of the air', we are not at all surprised to read that those meetings were characterized by a friendly and often even jovial atmosphere.

Sometimes such a meeting came about when a pilot who had forced down an adversary landed near him, introduced himself and started a conversation, as Immelmann did on the occasion of his first victory.* He did it again on 26 October 1915 when he scored his fifth victory. East of Arras he patiently stalked a

* See earlier.

Vickers FB5 of 11 Sqn RFC for a quarter of an hour before opening fire. The British crew were so completely surprised by the attack that the gunner did not fire a single shot. The Vickers was badly damaged by 40 hits, and the pilot, Captain C. C. Darley, who was wounded in the right arm, had no alternative but to come down in hostile territory. Immelmann landed beside them and went to meet them with great courtesy. The observer/gunner, Lieutenant R. L. Slade, who was not wounded, later wrote to his father from captivity: "Immelmann is a gentleman, and if ever we capture him I hope he will be treated the same."[2]

On 12 January 1916 Max Immelmann won his eighth victory. Near Bapaume he shot down another FB5 of 11 Sqn, in flames. The pilot, 2nd Lieutenant H. T. Kemp, succeeded in landing the plane and jumping out; his gunner, 2nd Lieutenant S. Hathaway, had died from a bullet wound in the abdomen. Immelmann landed in a nearby meadow and walked to the burning wreck to meet the pilot. They talked about their fight and Immelmann introduced himself and told his adversary that he was his eighth victim. When the British pilot heard who had defeated him, he said: "You are Immelmann? You are well known with us. Your victory today is another fine and sporting success for you."[3]

When the German pilot *Leutnant* Keller was brought down by the French pilot Gilbert on 10 January 1915 Gilbert gave his photograph to his victim and with it the written 'passport': "Memorable souvenir of an air combat. I beg French officers to treat kindly Lt. Keller, who was a gallant foe before he became a prisoner."[4]

Landing near your downed adversary was not without some risk, as Ernst Udet found out on 12 October 1916. He was then serving in *Jagdstaffel 15*, which had taken off in strength that day to intercept a large formation of French and British aircraft, out to bomb the Mauser factory at Oberndorf (Baden-Württemberg). Over Neubreisach *Jasta 15* attacked. Udet dived on a group of seven Breguet-Michelin IVs, belonging to *Escadrille BM. 120*. He opened fire on the leading bomber.

> The French pilot fell away and eventually made a forced landing, still intact. Udet immediately tried to land alongside his victim, hoping to prevent the bomber's crew destroying

General Ernst Udet in 1940, wearing both the Pour le Mérite *and the Knight's* Cross. *(Bundesarchiv)*

their machine, but his Fokker had suffered combat damage and a wheel tyre burst as he touched down, resulting in the Fokker tipping over onto its back.

Udet, uninjured, was helped from the Fokker by the French pilot, Maréchal de Logis Barlet, who was unwounded. His observer Luneau had been wounded in the left arm. . . . Udet shook hands with his latest victims, conversed politely for some minutes, and expressed his regret at having wounded Luneau. He later visited the Frenchmen in Mülhausen, each time taking cigarettes for them.[5]

It was Udet's second victory. Nearly two years later his 39th was another occasion on which he landed near an adversary he had just shot down. In the early morning of 2 July 1918 *Jasta 4* (one of the *Staffeln* of the famous *Jagdgeschwader Richthofen*), led by Udet, clashed with eight Nieuports of the 27th Aero Squadron of the US Air Service, near Chateau-Thierry. In the ensuing dogfight (in which *Jasta 10*, led by Erich Loewenhardt, joined) Udet shot down Lieutenant Walter B. Wanamaker's plane. He "landed near his victim, gave the wounded Wanamaker a cigarette, and asked him to autograph the patch of fabric with the Nieuport's serial number which had been cut from the aircraft tail".[6] He had the piece of fabric framed, and when he toured the United States in 1931 and met Wanamaker again, he gave it to him as a souvenir of their fight. Before that the two men had exchanged some letters; during this and Udet's subsequent visits to the States he and Wanamaker (who had become a judge in Akron, Ohio) became fast friends.[7]

More close friendships have developed between two former foes, friendships that originated in a face-to-face meeting on the ground after a grim duel in which they had shot at one another with clear intent to kill. One more example will suffice for the present.

On 1 August 1918 there was a tremendous air battle near Fère en Tardenois (about 25 miles west of Reims), in which the American 27th Aero Squadron suffered shattering losses at the hands of *Jagdstaffeln 17, 4, 6* and *10*, all first-rate units, the last three belonging to *Jagdgeschwader Richthofen*. Out of the eighteen pilots of the 27th Aero who were attacked while protecting two French Salmson reconnaissance aircraft, six

were killed and two were forced down and taken prisoner.*
One of these two was Lieutenant Charles A. McElvain.

> He fought a long duel with Lt. Alfred Fleischer, of *Jasta 17*,
> before running out of fuel and landing in German territory.
> As he glided in for a landing with a dead engine, Fleischer
> held his fire and landed beside him. The two became friends
> and after World War II, McElvain, then head of a mortgage
> company in Chicago, managed to bring Fleischer to the U.S.
> to live. The German pilot's son, now an American citizen, is
> employed by McElvain's firm.[8]

It did not often happen that a pilot was in a situation that he
could get into personal contact with an adversary in the open
field where his aircraft had landed or crashed. Sometimes,
however, other possibilities presented themselves for a meeting.

In the First World War it became the custom for both Allied
and German airmen to entertain in their messes enemy pilots
who had been brought down, before they had to deliver them
to the prisoner-of-war cages. On such occasions they had an
excellent opportunity to talk with their opponents and have a
good look at the men they only had caught glimpses of during
their encounters in the air. There was an understandable
curiosity about those strangers from another, hostile, world
who yet were kindred spirits. A curiosity that was also
apparent from the way pilots in the war looked at photographs
of their counterparts on the other side, and which was often
combined with wonder that their enemies were so much like
themselves. Comments were made like "They really are not
much different from us, are they? If it weren't for their
uniforms, they could pass for our boys."

Meeting them in the flesh, having them as guests, was an
exciting experience, which might reveal something about their
ideas and mentality. Questions were sometimes asked — what
their aircraft were like to fly, how many victories they had
won, whether they knew a certain top ace of theirs personally,
etc. But they often refrained from inquiring too intrusively, not
wanting to spoil the pleasant get-together by giving the
impression that they were trying to elicit secret military
information. That was not their job but the intelligence

* Among the ten who came home safe were Frank Luke and Joe Wehner
(see chapter 3). They had been posted to the 27th Aero Squadron only a
week before.

officer's. To be sure, there were also cases in which the hosts did try to make the captured man give away valuable secrets. Willie Fry (60 Sqn RFC) tells us that when, on 19 May 1917, he had brought down *Leutnant* Georg Noth of *Jasta Boelcke* near 60 Squadron's airfield, "my German pilot was brought in to luncheon and plied with drink on the chance that we might get some interesting information out of him. He did not say much and gave nothing away."[9]

On the other hand one finds remarks like this:

> Squadron binges took place on very exceptional occasions. . . . Infrequently, it was a request party in honor of some captured German airman. Rather like giving a condemned man anything his heart desires for his last meal. The brass hats always hoped the *spiritus frumenti* might loosen his tongue to the extent of disgorging information of real value. We always hoped they wouldn't, and they never did.[10]

Another man who was graciously entertained by his adversaries after being taken prisoner was the American James Norman Hall. He was serving as a sergeant pilot in the legendary *Escadrille Lafayette*[11] when this was incorporated into the US Air Service in February 1918 and became the 103rd Aero Squadron. Hall was commissioned as a captain in the USAS and remained with the 103rd Aero until 29 March, when he was assigned to the 94th Aero Squadron (soon to be known as the 'Hat-in-the-Ring' squadron*), as a flight commander. On the morning of 7 May 1918 he took off with two others to intercept enemy aircraft that had been reported approaching the lines. One of his companions was Rickenbacker, still a tyro then, but destined to become America's Ace of Aces. When, ten minutes later, near Pont-à-Mousson, they spied an Albatros two-seater spotting for the German artillery, and were about to attack it, the sharp-eyed Rickenbacker noticed four Pfalz fighters climbing towards them. He signalled to draw his mates' attention to the new situation, and the three Americans attacked the fighters instead.[12] In the dive a large part of the fabric of the upper wing of Hall's plane tore loose. He broke off his attack and set off for home. He did not get very far. A

---

* The aeroplanes of the squadron were marked on the sides of the fuselage by an "Uncle Sam's hat" in a ring, symbolizing the entry of the United States into the war.

The American ace Captain Eddie Rickenbacker in his Nieuport 28. Note the
"Hat-in-the-Ring" insignia of the 94th Aero Squadron. (Smithsonian Institute)

German anti-aircraft battery scored a direct hit in Hall's engine
and, though the shell did not explode, it stopped the engine.
Hall lost control and crashed behind the German lines. He
survived with a broken nose and ankle. He was soon
surrounded by a crowd of curious Germans, who behaved
towards him with utmost courtesy, treated his nose and put his
leg in splints. Shortly afterwards some flying officers arrived,
who gently aided him into a car and took him to their
aerodrome at Mars-le-Tour.

> He was shown every courtesy by the young pilots, who even
> forbore to ask him questions, though Jimmy knew they were
> burning up with curiosity. He wanted to talk to them, but
> didn't dare, for fear of revealing some information of value,
> so their conversation was limited to generalities.
>
> They kept him for lunch, played the piano for him and
> acted in every way as genial hosts. There was no bitterness in
> their recital of the fact that Rickenbacker and the other pilot
> had returned safely to their lines, but had succeeded in
> bringing down one of their comrades in flames during the
> fight. Jimmy felt a lot better, since the score was evened.

After lunch he was questioned by a major of intelligence, but gave out no information, and there was no resentment. Then the pilots took him to the hospital in a squadron car.

A day or two later one of them made a trip of thirty kilometers to the scene of Jim's wreck to get his helmet and gloves that he had forgotten. That was real chivalry, but they carried it even further. Hall asked them if they could drop a note over, advising his friends of his safety. One of the chaps very graciously volunteered to take it and was himself shot down and made prisoner as a result.[13]

After the war James N. Hall continued the literary work he had been doing before he enlisted in the French Aviation Corps. Together with his wartime friend Charles B. Nordhoff he edited a two-volume history of the *Escadrille Lafayette* (*The Lafayette Flying Corps*, Boston 1920). The two men travelled to Tahiti in the Pacific Ocean and they both settled in the island. Hall wrote a large number of books there, nearly half of them in collaboration with Nordhoff, the best known being *Mutiny on the Bounty*.

From the several personal accounts of pilots who have been received as honoured guests by their adversaries I have chosen the following: by (then Lieutenant) Duncan Grinnell-Milne of 16 Sqn RFC because, rather than recounting the bare facts, he gives us an insight into his emotions. When on 1 December 1915 he and his observer, Captain C. C. Strong, were returning from a long reconnaissance to Valenciennes, their BE2c developed engine trouble and they had to land in enemy territory. They set fire to their aeroplane, threw their maps and notes into the flames, and awaited the arrival of the Germans they saw approach, to surrender themselves.

The men who presently advanced towards us were from a German air squadron stationed less than a mile away. In a short time we were surrounded by a dozen or more young flying officers.

I have today no warmer a feeling of friendship, no greater a respect or admiration, no deeper an understanding of the men of the German Flying Corps than I had on the day of my capture. And this for the very good reason that in the course of one winter's afternoon in 1915 I learnt so to appreciate their qualities that no mode or trend of opinion can ever change my sentiments. They did much more than spare our lives; they spared our pride. With fellow-feeling for airmen in distress they solaced our despair. Towards us, captives from an alien and hated race, they made no gesture of anger or of reproach. Their hands were raised; but to salute us. They spoke to us not with words of triumph, or wrath or of scorn, but with a ready sympathy for our plight, a knowledge of all that our misfortune must mean to us. We were their enemies, British, and at their mercy; but they did not show by word or deed that they were aware of the fact. It may have been wholly that much-exaggerated "comradeship of the air" which linked us, but I prefer to believe that our mutual understanding ran deeper. We wore the uniforms of our respective countries, we stood for different causes, but, beneath all the superficialities, we knew that we were actuated by the same motives. Youth, adventure, high spirits — those things wound up for us the mainspring of life. We would have fought just as well without propaganda; we had no need for bitter hatred. So may it have been in the days of chivalry."[14]

In May 1918 Grinnell-Milne succeeded in escaping from captivity. He returned to England, was retrained in the RAF, and served the last few months of the war as a flight commander in the famous 56 Sqn, flying SE5a fighters and becoming an ace with six victories. Apparently he had not been treated as courteously in the POW camp as he had in the flying officers' mess just after his capture, for he painted the name *SCHWEINHUND* on the nose of his personal aircraft. "I can't remember exactly why I chose this name, except that I had been called it so often and that now most of my work was being done at an altitude where the Germans could read it plainly . . ." There was in the RAF an order against adding personal touches to the paintwork of aircraft, but Grinnell-Milne made light of that. When the squadron commander strolled up to his machine and asked "Hullo — why the paintwork? And what does that name mean?"

I tried to explain that it was meant to be a bit of "frightfulness" to annoy the Germans, and that in addition I hoped soon to have sketched out a portrait of the Kaiser on the radiator, painted so that when the shutters [in front of the radiator] were opened and closed rapidly the Imperial moustaches would wiggle and the eyes blink — the idea

131

being that a picture of the All Highest might put the enemy machine-gunners off their aim.[15]

However courteously and hospitably a captured pilot was treated by his adversaries, however hard they tried to make the gathering in their mess companionable, the man who had just lost his freedom could hardly be really at ease in the strange surroundings. He had recently gone through a traumatic experience; sometimes he was wounded and in pain. He would constantly have to be on his guard against saying anything that might be of military value to the enemy. His thoughts would be with his comrades who would by then have returned home, sitting in *their* mess, discussing what had happened, perhaps uncertain abut his fate. Above all, he would be fully aware that this comparative pleasantness was of short duration, that before long he would be turned over to a prisoner-of-war camp, where he would not be treated so kindly.

Little wonder that, in spite of a mutual will to please, the atmosphere at those gatherings was often rather strained. And yet there were humorous episodes, too.

The Australian Sir Gordon Taylor tells us a story he heard in July 1917, from a pilot of a neighbouring squadron on the British front in France, where Taylor himself served in 66 Sqn RFC. "It was a typical instance of the chivalrous relationship which generally existed between fallen opponents and their captors in the air forces on both sides." They had forced a German pilot down on the British side of the lines. He was

taken to the aerodrome of the squadron concerned. There he was treated as a guest, and that night entertained in the Officers' Mess.

After getting rid of his suspicions about this hospitable reception, a softening-up possibly aided by the good French wine, the German pilot enjoyed the occasion for what it was — a spontaneous gesture of goodwill to an unfortunate opponent. Towards the end he asked if he might be allowed to speak, and this wish of course was granted.

Speaking English, he first of all thanked his hosts for their warm hospitality to an enemy airman. Then he said that there in the Mess this night he hoped he would be understood in saying he felt that they were all, primarily, people of the air, though they happened to be at war. Then, drawing himself up formally, he said, 'I wish to give you a toast,' and, raising his glass, 'I give you "Hals und Beinbruch".'

There was a momentary silence in the Mess, and he went on, 'You see, in the German Air Force we think it is bad luck to wish you good luck; so to bring good luck we say "Hals und Beinbruch", "May you break your neck and legs".'

It went over well. History does not record the rest of the evening; but when, the next day, the inevitable processes for a prisoner-of-war had gone into action and he was escorted away, there was a feeling that if this deadly game had to be played, it was better played in a civilized manner."[16]

There is a lot of humour in a story in Ernst Udet's autobiography, about being hosts to a captured adversary. In the morning of 12 August 1918 Lothar von Richthofen*, commander of *Jasta 11* (in which Udet served then) brought down two British planes in quick succession. The last one, a Sopwith Camel, was also his very last (40th) victory, as he was wounded in combat the next day and remained convalescent for the rest of the war. The pilot of this Camel, a Major Summers, came down alive. Lothar met him and took him to the mess at Bernes aerodrome for the evening meal, introducing him to his pilots. Udet describes him as a lanky, somewhat nonchalant yet sportsmanlike man, amiable but with reserve, "in short: a gentleman".

We chat about horses, dogs and aeroplanes. Not about the war. The Englishman is our guest and he should not have the feeling that we are drawing him out.

In the middle of the conversation he whispers something to his neighbour, gets up and goes outside.

With some concern Lothar watches him go.

"Where does he want to go?"

"He asked 'I beg your pardon, where is the W.C.?' Mausezahn answers.

There is a short embarrassed silence. The outdoor privy is nearly three minutes' walk away. Behind it is a wood. For a sportsman it is not difficult to escape from there.

Opinions vary. Maushake is the most resolute. He wants to go out, too, and station himself beside the Englishman. This can be done in a natural way. But Lothar objects. "So far we have treated the man as a guest, and he has given us no occasion to doubt his decency."

But an uneasiness remains. After all, we are responsible

* One of Manfred's two brothers, his junior by two years.

for the prisoner. If he gets away, there will be a frightful row.

One of us goes to the window and follows the Englishman with his eyes. Promptly six or eight follow suit and group around him. I among them.

The Englishman strides across the field. He stops, lights a cigarette, looks around him. We immediately squat down. Hospitality is sacred, and our distrust could offend him.

He disappears behind the deal wall of the privy.

This does not extend all the way to the ground, you can see his brown boots. That is reassuring.

But Maushake's detective instinct has been roused.

"Look fellows," he says breathlessly, "he does not stand there in his boots any longer. He has climbed over the back wall in his stockings and has run away. The boots simply cannot stand like that if . . .".

He shows us how legs actually should stand during this process.

The Englishman reappears from behind the wall. Stooping deeply we slink back to our places. When he comes in we are chatting about horses, dogs and aeroplanes.

"I should never have forgiven myself if I had disappointed such hosts," the English major says, a little smile touching the corners of his mouth. We thank him earnestly and solemnly.

The next morning a small soldier with a bushy beard collects the prisoner. He turns round a few times and waves to us."

Five days later they hear that an English prisoner has overpowered his escort and has escaped in a German uniform. From the toilet of a running corridor train. They have found his escort locked in the toilet.

"Was it a major?" Mausezahn asks excitedly.
"It was indeed an English major of the flying corps."
"So from the W.C. after all!" cries Mausezahn.
We laugh till our jaws are hurting.[17]

Another possibility of meeting adversaries socially was to go and visit them in hospital. Oswald Boelcke did this on 7 January 1916. On the 5th he had attacked a British two-seater north-east of Hénin Liétard. In the ensuing fight he wounded both the observer and the pilot, who signalled him by hand that he wished to surrender. Boelcke followed them down warily, firing some warning shots now and then. When the British plane had come down (breaking up because a control wire had been severed) Boelcke landed nearby. When he arrived at the crash site quite a crowd had already gathered round. The crew's wounds were being bandaged by two medical orderlies. Boelcke shook hands with his victims and told them he was glad he had got them down alive. He had a long conversation with the pilot, who spoke good German. When he heard Boelcke's name he grinned and said, "We know it well". Two days later Boelcke visited the observer in hospital (the pilot had already been discharged and transported to a POW camp) and brought him some English magazines and also a few photographs of the wreck of their aircraft.[18]

When Max Immelmann had brought down a British two-seater near Douai on 2 March 1916 (his 9th victory) he visited the pilot (Lieutenant Palmer) in hospital on the same day. The observer had been killed.[19]

There are several more instances on record of pilots visiting their victims in hospital[20], or even in prison[21] in the First World War. From the fact that there are rather more stories about Germans calling on Allied captives than the other way round, it should not be concluded that the Allied airmen were less disposed to extend that particular courtesy than their enemies. There is not any reason for such a supposition. Apart from pure coincidence, a possible explanation may lie in the fact that in the First World War more Allied than German planes came down on the wrong side of the front lines. This was mainly caused by the prevailing westerly (and often strong) winds in northern France and Belgium. A natural phenomenon that was, of course, of great advantage to the Germans and partly determined their tactics.

So far in this chapter I have only dealt with cases in the 1914-1918 War. As we have seen in chapter 1, chivalrous behaviour was less often found in the Second World War. But a number of interesting accounts of more or less friendly encounters between airmen of opposing sides convince us that courteous and friendly behaviour was the rule rather than the exception in such situations.

Sometimes it was just a short meeting, such as Squadron Leader A. D. Farquhar (602 Sqn RAF) had on 22 February

Johannes "Macky" Steinhoff, who was to end the war with 176 victories, in his Messerschmitt Bf 109, when he was still a Hauptmann *(Captain), in 1942.*

(Bundesarchiv)

1940 with the crew of a Heinkel He 111 bomber he had attacked and forced down near St. Abb's Head in Berwickshire.

> The Heinkel landed, and Farquhar saw the crew climbing out. It then occurred to him that they would probably set fire to their machine, and he thought that would be a pity. He decided to go down and prevent them doing so. But when the Spitfire landed alongside the Heinkel its wheels bogged in marshy ground and the fighter turned right over on its back.
>
> Farquhar, held by his shoulder straps, hung ingloriously upside down with his nose a few inches from Scottish soil. The next thing of which he was aware was a pair of hands gripping him while others released his harness. His rescuers stood smiling. They were the Germans he had shot out of the sky a few minutes before."[22]

At other times the adversaries had an opportunity of getting to know one another more closely. During the Italian campaign in the autumn of 1943, *Oberst* Johannes Steinhoff,

then commanding *Jagdgeschwader 77**, shot down a Lockheed
P-38. He landed immediately, found the American pilot and
put him up for the night in his own tent. Steinhoff's men
wanted to tie up the American with rope and attach a string to
their *Kommodore*'s toe. But Steinhoff asked him if he would
give his word of honour that he would not run away, and the
American agreed. They drank a considerable amount of
Schnaps together, and then

> two enemies who only a few hours before had been trying to
> blast each other from the air with batteries of cannon and
> machine-guns lay down and slept side by side in the same
> tent, bound only by the ancient military tradition of parole.
>
> Next morning, the two men had breakfast together. They
> both had bad hangovers and consumed a large amount of
> black coffee.[23]

With understandable regret the American pilot had to leave
Steinhoff's hospitality for the POW camp.

Eduard Neumann, *Kommodore* of *Jagdgeschwader 27* in
North Africa in 1942, has this to say about the relations
between his pilots and enemy pilots whom they met as
prisoners-of-war:

> Many German pilots could speak English better than any
> other foreign language and were thus always quickly on good
> terms with captured pilots. We endeavoured always to be as
> hospitable as possible in order to make their passage into
> captivity a little less bitter. We were again and again
> impressed to see how the captured pilots tried to conceal
> their regret and feign indifference and frivolity. For example,
> one time a very young Australian Flying Officer was rescued
> by the chief of our Desert Rescue Staffel immediately after
> landing in mid desert. When he got out of the [Fieseler]
> Fi.156 he said to us with a bright smile: 'What a good
> service!'[24]

From the other side in the same theatre of war comes the
following statement, written by Ralph J. 'Doc' Watson, who
served as a Captain in the 48th Squadron, 14th FG, USAAF,
in the North African desert:

---

* After the war, Johannes 'Macky' Steinhoff had an important share in the
work of building up the new German Air Force, whose Inspector he
ultimately became. General Steinhoff also served in high NATO posts.

Upon visiting the captured German pilots in the French jail, I was amazed how much they seemed like us. Any one of them could have been an American. I think that they were pretty much gentlemen and fought fairly and rendered an adequate account of themselves on all occasions in which I was involved. I still feel kindly towards the German pilots and when one compares them with the treatment received in Vietnam and Korea, it makes them appear even higher in my esteem."[25]

The custom in the First World War to entertain captured enemy pilots before they had to be sent on their way to the POW camps was continued in the Second World War, if only in Europe and North Africa, among the German airmen on the one side and British and American airmen on the other.

On 24 November 1939, during the so-called 'phoney war'*, 1 Sqn RAF, equipped with Hawker Hurricane fighters, destroyed two Dornier Do 17s over north-east France. One was attacked by a section led by Cyril D. Palmer, from Cleveland, Ohio, who had joined the RAF before the war. One of the Dornier's engines was set on fire and the bomber lost height, appearing to be more or less out of control. Two of the German crew baled out, but not the pilot. When Palmer flew alongside to investigate, he saw him slumped in his seat, his head lolled to one side. But this was a ruse. Suddenly the German throttled back, swerved on Palmer's tail and raked the Hurricane with machine-gun fire, damaging it so severely that Palmer had to make a belly-landing. Meanwhile the two other British pilots renewed the attack on the German who, with both engines on fire now, had to force-land too. The pilot got out safely and waved to the Hurricanes circling over the crash site.

The Dornier was found to have at least 500 bullet holes in it — not enough, considering that three Hurricanes had had a go at it. Apparently the pilot had had to leave his seat to lock the gun with which he had shot Pussy [Palmer] down. We all felt that this German had put up a damned good show, and as a tribute to the spirit that all pilots admire, we determined to have him to dine with us as a guest. The French authorities were very reluctant to part with him, but eventually he was

* The period of inactivity (on land) on the Western Front, before the German offensive started on 10 May 1940 (the *Blitzkrieg*), is often called the 'phoney war'. The Germans spoke of the *Sitzkrieg* and the French of *drôle de guerre*.

allowed to come with Hilly, whom we had sent to fetch him.

He turned out to be a non-commissioned officer of some experience. Suspicious at first, he melted as he realized our goodwill, and we gave him the best dinner we could muster under the circumstances. Everything went very well except for one awkward incident. Mistaking Hilly's laughter at a joke for amusement at his plight, the German got very serious, and then suddenly broke down. We all understood that he must be now a little overwrought after his ordeal in the air and his capture, so were not as surprised as we might otherwise have been. On being taken outside he quickly pulled himself together — adding to his apologies the explanation that he was fed up with the war. He left us at 1 a.m. — all of us being by then pretty merry — the richer by several articles of warm clothing, and vainly requesting that he should be sent to England in between assurances that we would be treated with equal kindness should we be taken prisoner by his countrymen."[26]

Hauptmann Wilhelm Balthasar, one of the early German aces in the Second World War, with combat experience in the Spanish Civil War, enjoyed having conversations with RAF fighter pilots who had been taken prisoner. He would have them brought to his mess for a drink, a meal and an exchange of views on military aviation matters. One day at the end of June 1941 Balthasar acted as host to a young British pilot, who in the course of the conversation stated positively that he knew that Ernst Udet had committed suicide by shooting himself in the head with a pistol. Which is exactly what happened . . . more than four months later! By that time Balthasar was dead too, shot down by RAF fighters and killed, on 3 July 1941.[27]

Another German ace who liked entertaining captured enemy pilots was Wolfgang Falck. He had gained early — if rather disproportionate — fame from his participation in the Battle of the Heligoland Bight on 18 December 1939, the first encounter in strength between a formation of RAF bombers and *Luftwaffe* fighters in the Second World War. On that cold and sunny day 22 Vickers Wellingtons were on an armed reconnaissance of those waters. They were picked up by two German radar stations. But when their operators reported the British formation they met with a disbelief that matches the reaction the American radar operator on northern Oahu got,

Wolfgang Falck at the controls of his Messerschmitt Bf 110 at Jever airbase in January 1940.
Colour drawing by Prof. Wolfram Wilrich.   *(Falck Collection)*

two years later, when he reported a large formation of aircraft heading for Pearl Harbor. "Tommies coming over in weather

140

like this? You must be plotting seagulls or there's interference on your set!"[28] Only after a visual sighting report had been received did the *Luftwaffe* send up fighters. They were in time to intercept the unfortunate Wellingtons on their way home. Sixteen Bf 110s and 34 Bf 109s proceeded to slaughter the British aircraft. Only eight of them returned to their home bases.[29] In a cruel way the RAF had learned the lesson that bombers without fighter escort could not survive in daylight operations, a lesson the *Luftwaffe* learned in the Battle of Britain and the USAAF in 1943, over Germany.

The German propaganda machine made the most of the great victory. Three officers were selected to play the leading roles in films, broadcasts and numerous illustrated newspaper and magazine articles. They were *Oberstleutnant* Carl Schuhmacher, *Kommodore* of *JG 1*, *Oberleutnant* Johannes Steinhoff*, who had flown one of the Messerschmitt Bf 109s, and *Oberleutnant* Wolfgang Falck, the pilot of one of the Messerschmitt Bf 110s.[30]

The Germans circulated and broadcast the story of their victory throughout Europe, and in Britain several people recognized Falck. The editor of the British aviation periodical *The Aeroplane*, who had met him several times before the war, told his readers, in the 1 March 1940 issue, what the German pilot was like:

> He looks like a falcon. He is not big enough to be an eagle.
> But he has the aquiline features which artists and novelists
> love to ascribe to heroic birdmen. He speaks excellent
> English and is a charming companion.

He was indeed a most charming man, as several of his adversaries could attest who experienced his hospitality after being taken prisoners.

He tells of a Spitfire pilot whose oxygen system had failed over Holland and in the resulting dazed state had landed on the German base at Deelen. After Falck had entertained him in the officers' club, he had him flown to Frankfurt in the rear seat of a Messerschmitt Bf 110, which was a great treat for the British pilot. He telephoned Falck from Frankfurt to thank him for the ride and hospitality.[31]

* We have met Steinhoff, as *Oberst*, at a later stage of the war, on page 135.

Oberst Falck was *Kommodore* of a night-fighter *Geschwader* then, *NJG 1*. In that same period he once treated five crewmen of a downed RAF bomber to lunch at his headquarters in Arnhem. The Englishman seated at Falck's right hand was withdrawn and obviously apprehensive.

> 'He didn't dare to eat his soup,' Falck recalls with a smile. 'He was afraid it was poisoned. So I explained to him that we were all soldiers together, and that we were all under discipline in our Air Force as he was in his. I offered to change soup with him as assurance against poisoning.'
>
> The RAF man finally succumbed to the Falck charm, ate his soup [and] warmed up to the young Germans around him. [. . .] After lunch, he and Falck took a stroll through a beautiful little garden which Falck maintained on the base and the two former enemies admired its lushness together."[32]

Gerhard Schöpfel, one of the most successful German fighter pilots in the Battle of Britain, tells a story of an American volunteer in the RAF (he gives his name as Clarke) who was brought down in France in 1940. He had blazing red hair, and, curiously enough, the young *Feldwebel* who defeated him also had a shock of red hair. The RAF pilot made a belly landing and jumped out of his plane, pulling off his helmet just as the German flew low over him. Astounded to see that his late adversary had the same red hair as he had, the *Feldwebel* flew home and told Schöpfel, his commanding officer, about it. "That evening we brought Clarke to our base and the two redheads met on the ground."[33]

Schöpfel was also present at the famous meeting, in August 1941, between two legendary fighter pilots, Douglas Bader and Adolf Galland.

Bader was a promising young fighter pilot in 23 Sqn RAF when, in December 1931, while stunt flying a Bristol Bulldog low over Woodley aerodrome, near Reading, his left wing-tip touched the ground and he crashed. The frightful accident led to the loss of both his legs. He very nearly lost his life, too. Bader has said that hearing a nurse say, "Sssh! Don't make so much noise. There's a boy dying in there" saved his life. It snapped him out of a lethargy from which he might well have slipped into death. With incredible courage and will-power he overcame all seemingly insurmountable obstacles that stand in the way of a man without legs who wants to recover his ability to walk (without crutches or even a stick), to drive a car and, above all, to fly an aeroplane — and keep his sanity in the process. The exceptional physical fitness he had, helped of course. Six months after the accident he could walk again unaided, on artificial legs. A few months later he got an opportunity to demonstrate that he was still a capable pilot. But in spite of this he was invalided out of the service. The regulations simply did not cover a case like his. When war came a new situation arose. Good friends in high positions exerted some influence and the rules were bent. Bader was restored to the active list, sent to the Central Flying School for a refresher course and, in February 1940, was posted back again to a fighter squadron, No.19, equipped with Spitfires.[34] Bader gained rapid promotion. After a few months he was appointed a Flight Commander in 222 Sqn, with which he won his first victory, a Bf 109 on 1 June 1940. Then, at the end of that month, he was given command of 242 (Canadian) Squadron, which had just come back from the Battle of France in complete disorder and utterly demoralized. Within a few weeks Bader managed to regenerate the squadron and mould it into a well-trained, spirited and aggressive unit, in time for the Battle of Britain.

It was not long after winning that battle, in fact before the year was out, that RAF Fighter Command went on the offensive, regularly crossing the Channel into northern France, mostly acting as cover for small groups of bombers. It was on one of these raids that Douglas Bader was shot down and taken prisoner.

In March 1941 he had become one of the first two wing leaders, commanding the Tangmere wing. On the morning of 9 August his wing took off for a target support mission to Béthune, 20 miles south-west of Lille. When they crossed the French coast just south of Le Touquet they sighted a dozen Messerschmitt Bf 109s below them and attacked. Bader — for once — bungled his own attack and found himself isolated from the others. He then saw three pairs of 109s in front of him, apparently unaware of the lone Spitfire near them. He attacked and shot down one of the centre pair and had just opened fire on the other when he saw two 109s on his left curving towards him. Then Bader made his final mistake: instead of turning towards these attackers (one of Oswald Boelcke's rules!), he turned away from them. With a terrific bang something hit him, and the controls became slack. He looked behind and got the impression that the whole of the Spitfire's tail was missing. He must have collided with another 109 he thought. With considerable difficulty he extricated himself from the cockpit of the madly gyrating plane, was dragged out by the force of the airstream and parachuted down. His right artificial leg was left behind in the cockpit. While he was floating down "he heard engine noises and turned in the harness. A Messerschmitt was flying straight at him, but the pilot did not shoot. He turned and roared by fifty yards away."[35] With his one artificial leg he hit the ground rather clumsily and he was knocked unconscious. When he came to, two German soldiers were bending over him, removing his parachute harness. They took him to the hospital in St. Omer in a car.

The next morning two young *Luftwaffe* pilots came to visit him. One of them was Graf (Count) Erbo von Kageneck. The conversation was in English.

> Bader was fairly monosyllabic but the Germans chatted amiably. Would he like some books? They'd just come over from St. Omer airfield to yarn as one pilot to another. Spitfires were jolly good aeroplanes.
>
> "Yes," Bader said. "So are yours."
>
> After a while the Count said politely: "I understand you have no legs?" He was looking at the fore-shortened form under the bedclothes.
>
> "That's right."
>
> They asked what it was like flying without legs.[36]

Later that day Bader asked a German engineering officer who came to see him whether it would be possible to send a radio message to England, asking them to send another leg for him. And would they please search the wreckage of his Spitfire for the leg he had lost while getting out of it? The German promised to do what he could. The leg was indeed found. It was much damaged of course, but the Germans did a magnificent repair job on it. Now Bader was able to walk about again, and at once he began making plans to escape.

Four days later the two young flying officers visited him

again, this time bringing two bottles of champagne, which helped to make it a cheery little party.

> The Count had obviously shot down some British aircraft but was too polite to mention that or to ask how many Bader had shot down*. In fact, neither he nor his comrade asked any dangerous questions, but chatted gaily about their own tactics and aeroplanes. [. . .] Bader liked them both; they were 'types' after his own heart and he would have liked to have had them in his wing. What a damn' silly war it was.[37]

Through these officers Bader also received a message from *Oberstleutnant* Adolf Galland, *Kommodore* of *JG 26*. This was the *Jagdgeschwader* which Bader's wing had so often become involved with in aerial combat, as it had on 9 August, when *JG 26* had lost two of three aircraft against the Tangmere wing's two. Galland sent his compliments and invited Bader to come and have tea with him and his officers at their headquarters and airfield near Wissant.

> Bader was intrigued. It would be churlish to refuse, and in any case he would love to meet Galland (probably they had already met in the air). It brought a breath of the chivalry lost from modern war. And it was a chance to spy out the country, to see the other side, life on an enemy fighter station, to weigh it up and compare it. Might get back home with a 109!
> "I'd be delighted to come," he said.[38]

Adolf Galland was one of the best-known German fighter pilots in the Second World War. His name certainly ranks with the greatest, of both sides, in both world wars. Earlier in this book we have already met him twice,* once replying to a tentative question by Göring, and a second time winning his first aerial victories, in May 1940. He had had his baptism of fire long before that, however, in the Spanish Civil War, serving with the *Legion Condor*, but not as a fighter pilot. He did fly fighter aircraft in Spain, Heinkel He 51s, but they had become obsolete and were then only used as ground attack aircraft in direct support of the army. In the Polish campaign in 1939 he again flew ground attack aircraft, Henschel Hs 123s this time. It was not until the fighting in Poland was over that

* Bader was officially credited with 23 victories.
* On pages 53 and 55.

August 1941. Wing-Commander Douglas Bader as a prisoner of war, being received by Oberstleutnant *Adolf Galland,* Kommodore *of JG 26, and his officers at their headquarters. Galland is third from left, and the man holding gloves in his left hand is* Oberst *Joachim Huth, a World War I pilot who had lost a leg in that war.* (Via Galland)

his long-cherished wish was granted to be re-transferred to a fighter unit.

From then on he rapidly climbed into prominence. In June 1940, he was given command of *III./JG 26* (the 3rd group of *Jagdgeschwader 26*) and two months later was assigned to command the whole *Geschwader*. On 21 June 1941 he was the first member of any of the armed forces to be awarded the Swords to the Knight's Cross. In the meantime his victory tally went up steadily, too. By the middle of August, when Galland received Bader, he had shot down more than 70 enemy aircraft.

It was a sunny day when a German officer and a sergeant called for Bader at the St. Omer hospital, from where he was driven the 15 miles to Audembert in the *Kommodore*'s big official car, a Horch, which Galland hardly ever used. When it stopped in front of the officers' mess, Galland stepped forward, put out his hand and introduced himself and then the others who were present.

146

Although everyone knew it was strictly forbidden for them to interrogate prisoners — this was to be left to the specialists at the interrogation centres — Galland had nevertheless instructed them to avoid even the semblance of questioning their guest on military matters. Bader was on his guard anyhow, and reticent about what could conceivably be of use to the Germans, even about such a seemingly innocent matter as his personal victory score. When they asked him what it was, he would not be more precise than "Oh, not many," evading further questions on the subject by saying it really was not worth talking about his victories, which were so few compared with those of Galland and Mölders. "And perhaps it was indeed only modesty that he did not want to speak of it in our presence," writes Galland.[39] In the course of the conversation Bader unbent a little. He was shown an elaborate model railway, which was the *Kommodore*'s favourite diversion when not flying. After playing with it for some time, Galland offered to show him round the field, and Bader gladly accepted the invitation. After walking several hundred yards along hedges and through a coppice on the skilfully camouflaged ground, they came to an aircraft pen. In it stood Galland's Messerschmitt Bf 109.

> Bader looked at it fascinated, and Galland made a polite gesture for him to climb in. He surprised them by the way he hauled himself on to the wing-root, grabbed his right leg and swung it into the cockpit and climbed in unaided. As he cast a glinting professional eye over the cockpit lay-out Galland leaned in and pointed things out.[40]

"I was pleased with the great interest and comprehension this splendid pilot showed. He would be a fine member of our 'club'!"[41] With these words Galland voiced the same feelings as Bader did about the German officers who visited him in hospital.

After Galland's explanations Bader asked him if he would do him a great favour and allow him to make a short flight round the airfield in the Messerschmitt. Clearly, it was impossible for Galland to consent to that. He said, "I'm afraid that if I should grant your request you would make an effort to escape. I should then be obliged to take off after you. After having just become acquainted we wouldn't want to shoot at one another again." Bader laughed and no more was said about it. One wonders if it crossed their minds that Bader might give — or be asked to give — his word of honour not to escape.

There is an amusing side issue to this episode. One of the many photographs that were taken during Bader's visit to the German airfield shows him sitting in the cockpit of the Messerschmitt, with Galland standing on the wing, leaning towards him. In the foreground is an officer holding what seems to be a pistol. When Bader saw the photograph after the war he concluded that all the time he had sat in the cockpit this officer had been ready to shoot him if he tried to escape. A rather naïve idea. As if the Germans did not have several much simpler means of blocking such an attempt, if only by preventing the engine from being started, or, if that should fail, by hindering the aircraft taxiing from the pen to the aerodrome, of which Bader, from where he sat, "could see no signs".[42] What the officer held in his left hand, resting on his hip, were his gloves. He was *Oberst* Joachim Huth, a veteran of the First World War, who had lost a leg in that conflict and now had a wooden one. As a result he was not too steady when standing, which is why he often gave himself a better balance by resting his hand on his hip.

Galland had noticed that Bader's right leg — the one that had crashed with the Spitfire and had been provisionally repaired — "creaked and clanked like a small armoured car". Bader repeated to him his request to make a signal to England, asking them to send a good right leg for him. Galland promised Bader that he would actively attend to the matter.

He asked and immediately received Göring's permission to get into radio contact with the RAF about Bader and his requirement. The international wavelength for distress signals at sea was used. Galland cannot now recall the exact wording of the message.[43] But in all probability the Germans actually made a tentative offer of a free passage for the aircraft in which the spare leg for Bader was to be flown across. RAF fighters could escort it part of the way and then Messerschmitts would take over. The British aircraft could land on an airfield near the coast and, after the leg had been handed over, take off again.[44] A most chivalrous gesture! Alas, the British did not think fit to react in kind. Apparently they were afraid that an arrangement as proposed by the Germans would be of great propaganda value to them. Soon afterwards, Bristol Blenheims bombed the *Luftwaffe* aerodromes in the Pas de Calais and other targets near St. Omer. In the course of these attacks they also dropped by parachute a yellow box, containing the artificial leg. Not sure, apparently, that it would be found, they confirmed by radio that it had been dropped.

Naturally, Galland and his men were greatly disappointed with the contentious British reaction to their well-meant proposal. They were not in a very tolerant mood as it was, because in the meantime Bader had escaped, and during the investigation that followed, Galland's unauthorized liberal reception of Bader came in for a good deal of criticism. He was reprimanded by Göring because of it and later commented: "It was bad for me."[45]

Bader had escaped from his room on the third floor of the hospital the very night after his visit to Galland. He got out by way of the window, lowering himself along a 'rope' made out of 15 bedsheets knotted together. Arrangements had been made through a local French girl working in the hospital. That night a young Frenchman met Bader at the hospital gate and helped him walk to the home of an elderly couple who were to harbour him until he could be passed on to others, who would try to get him back to England. But the next day he was caught again; another hospital worker had betrayed the address where he was hiding to the Germans. A year later Bader made his second and only other really serious attempt at escape, from a prison camp.[46] It was unsuccessful. After having been moved from one camp to another, he ultimately arrived at the special camp for would-be escapers at Colditz Castle, some 30 miles from Dresden. Here he was liberated by the United States First Army, on 5 April 1945.

Three weeks later — on 26 April; Germany had not capitulated yet — Adolf Galland made his last sortie of the war, leading a force of six Messerschmitt Me 262 jet fighters of *Jagdverband 44* from München-Riem. One of the Me 262s had to turn back with engine trouble. The remainder intercepted and attacked a force of Martin B-26 Marauder bombers of the 1st Tactical Air Force, flown by French crews, near Neuburg

August 1941. Douglas Bader is allowed to sit in the cockpit of a Messerschmitt Bf109. *(Via Galland)*

an der Donau. Galland blew up one of them with a burst from his four 30mm cannon and scored a few hits on another. Trying to see what had happened to the second bomber, he was surprised by an escort fighter, a Republic P-47 Thunderbolt of 50th FG, flown by Lieutenant James Finnegan, who seriously damaged the jet fighter and wounded Galland in the right knee. Galland broke off the action and managed to escape and return to Riem. Immediately after landing he had to clamber quickly out of the cockpit and dive into one of the many bomb craters in the field, because it was just being strafed by Thunderbolts and Lightnings. The end of the war saw him in hospital.[47]

Since his meeting with Bader in August 1941 a great deal had happened to Galland. When in November of that year Werner Mölders was killed in an accident, Göring appointed Galland as his successor, to *General der Jagdflieger*. With the actual rank of *Oberst* (Colonel), it became his task to inspect the fighter units on all fronts. A year later he was promoted to

150

September 1970. Four new Honorary Citizens of the City of Winnipeg, Canada. From left: Adolf Galland, Douglas Bader, Johnny Fauquier, a Canadian pilot, and Johnnie Johnson, second ranking British ace of World War II. When the Mayor of Winnipeg presented the Freedom of the City to them, Bader, who was sitting next to Galland, muttered to him "I cannot think what have you done for the City of Winnipeg!" (Via Galland)

Generalmajor. At the age of 30, he was the youngest German general. In the course of 1944 the relations between Galland and Göring became more and more strained, because the *Reichsmarschall* repeatedly abused the fighter pilots, reproaching them with cowardice, no less! On one occasion feelings ran so high that Galland tore his Knight's Cross* from his neck and flung it before Göring on the table. He did not wear any decoration for more than six months. He fell into disfavour with Hitler, too, who in January 1945 dismissed him from the function of *General der Jagdflieger* and ordered him to

* By this time with Oak Leaves, Swords and Diamonds.

151

establish a special fighter unit equipped with Me 262 jet fighters. He could select his own pilots. Galland gathered round him former *Kommodores* and other unit leaders who had incurred Göring's or Hitler's disfavour (Johannes Steinhoff among them), and added a few other experienced pilots. This most remarkable group of great aces, officially designated *Jagdverband 44 (JV 44)*, did not become operational until 31 March 1945, so only a few weeks of fighting remained for them, a last upsurge of the fighting spirit of an élite group of men against hopeless odds, in a war that had been lost long before.

Shortly afterwards Galland met Bader again, at Tangmere airbase near Southampton. The tables were turned: this time Galland was a prisoner-of-war. Bader had brought a box of good cigars for him and most graciously concerned himself about him and his personal well-being.[48]

Galland and Bader became good friends after the war. They regularly met until Bader's death in 1982. In all their conversations one question was never cleared up: did Bader collide with a German fighter on that 9 August 1941, or was he shot down by one? Bader remained convinced that there had been a collision. Galland insists that he was shot down, that the rear part of the Spitfire must have been hit by 20 mm cannon shells from one of the Messerschmitt Bf 109s of *JG 26*. The tail had not come off, either. If it had, Galland says, the abandoned Spitfire could not have come down the way it did, in a kind of belly-landing.[49]

The friendship between Bader and Galland is only one example of the numerous good relationships that grew up between former adversaries after hostilities came to an end. International contacts became possible again and ever more easy. The comradeship of the air flourished again. It had never ceased to be alive, and indeed had sometimes proved stronger than official enmity.

For all their awareness of belonging to an international brotherhood, it was still surprising to the veterans how hospitably they were received by men they had done their best to kill only a short time ago, and how easily they could set aside the notion of having been on different sides of a bitter conflict. As Johannes Steinhoff once said after speaking on his war

August 1978. Former enemies having great fun together at an aviation meeting at Bex, near Montreux, in Switzerland. From left: Geoffrey Page, Adolf Galland, Robert Stanford Tuck and Douglas Bader, aces all, with a Swiss driver at the wheel. (Via Galland)

experiences to a group of American aces in Washington: "It is a strange world after all, where it is possible for a man who fought for years against you to be invited here to talk about his experiences. If someone had told me twenty years ago that this would happen today I would have considered him insane."[50]

Such is the power of chivalry.

7

Aircraft markings in the chivalric tradition

NO other machine of war in history has ever been adorned with such an abundance of various non-essential additions to its normal, functional paint scheme as the aeroplane. Part of these markings can be traced back to the jousts and tournaments in medieval times and can be said to be in the chivalric tradition.

It all began soberly enough. The earliest military aeroplanes were almost devoid of markings. Usually no more than an identity number or letter — and sometimes the manufacturer's name — was to be seen on them. At first most countries did not even consider an indication of the nationality of their aircraft necessary. The one exception was France, which introduced a national marking even before the First World War — in July 1912. It was in the form of a cockade, in the colours of the French national flag: blue, white and red.* Soon after the outbreak of hostilities the other belligerents also adopted national insignia, as a safeguard against their aeroplanes being shot at by both sides instead of only by the enemy. The Royal Flying Corps painted Union Jacks on the underside of the wings of their aeroplanes. This proved to be an unfortunate choice, because the Cross of St. George on the Union Jack was easily mistaken for the black "Iron Cross" which the Germans

---

* This cockade (French: *cocarde*) dates from the French Revolution. The regular army wore white cockades at the time, and when — after the fall of the Bastille in 1789 — the National Guard also wanted to wear cockades, the Marquis de Lafayette proposed combining white (regarded as the national colour then) with blue and red, the colours of Paris. His idea was adopted and he thus originated the *tricolore*.

had chosen for their national insignia. So, in December 1914, the British changed over to the cockade of their French allies, only reversing the order of the colours. This type of national marking, the roundel, was ultimately adopted by all the other Allied nations.

As the number of aeroplanes employed in the war grew, the air forces found it expedient to introduce unit markings as well. The RFC chose simple fuselage bands or geometrical figures in black or white; the French and especially the Germans opted for colourful, often symbolic motifs of every imaginable kind. Later still, pilots began adding personal markings to their aeroplanes' paint schemes, but not in the RFC, which did not allow this.

Identity marks were nothing new in war, of course. From the earliest times military forces had used them for recognition purposes. Quite often marks were chosen that had in the past served a merely decorative purpose. This was the case when in medieval times paintings on shields came to be used as identifying marks, for which there was a great need because by then the personal armour of the mounted warrior covered him from head to foot, making the man inside unrecognizable. The use of hereditary insignia of a knight or a nobleman for the purpose of identification was, in the 12th century, the origin of heraldry.[1] These heraldic devices were at first depicted on the shield only, but were soon displayed also on the surcoats of knights (hence "coat of arms") and on their horses' trappings.

It should not be thought, however, that the use of such devices was limited to truly heraldic, i.e. hereditary, ones. There is plenty of pictorial evidence that many devices were in use that cannot properly speaking be called heraldic, and that they were used ever more often.

"In order that we may appreciate to the full the heroic flavour and chivalrous significance of heraldry in its medieval heyday", Maurice Keen emphasizes two points.[2] The first is that

> it very rapidly came to be much more than a systematic aid to the recognition of combatants in the field. It was infused early with powerful overtones of pride of lineage and esteem for martial achievement. Recognition in the field had in itself implications beyond the merely practical level, with giving

courage its due meed. That is why Jacques de Hemricourt lamented the passing of the good old days when men wore full surcoats of arms and bore their shield in battle, for then 'none dared be a coward, for one could tell the good men from the bad by their blazons'. [. . .] In the case of the tournament (with which the origins of heraldry were so closely associated), the practical ends of military exercise and the end of celebrating the chivalrous values and virtues became in course of time indistinguishable; and in the same way in heraldry the practical ends of recognition and authentication and the chivalrous ideology of martial honour and virtue came to be inseparably interwoven with one another.

This brings Keen to the second point.

The significance of heraldry in the medieval past is often underrated by modern historians, and one principal reason for this is that we nowadays live with a literary culture which is far less dependent on the visual than was that of the middle ages.

To illustrate the importance of "the sign language of heraldry" in those times, Keen gives some examples of people being designated by their coats of arms, both in speech (e.g. "Commend me to my friend whose blazon is thus and thus") and in paintings depicting scenes of chivalrous history.

There is another aspect of medieval heraldry that needs to be brought up. Within certain limits it gave those who assumed a coat of arms — often upon no other authority than their own — an opportunity to follow their temperament, or even a whim, in choosing the design. In view of the importance of the play element in culture it is only natural that we also find it effective at this early stage in the development of heraldry. Arms were chosen that wittily made play with the name of the family, or referred to an episode in its history, or carried a hidden meaning. And one can imagine the artists and craftsmen who decorated the shields, surcoats and horses' trappings with the chosen design adding a few playful touches of their own. Later, more and more rules were laid down concerning heraldic devices, and this considerably hampered free expression, especially of playfulness.

When, some eight centuries later, the coming of the war in

the air was attended with a revival of the spirit of chivalry, the 20th-century knights of the air took a leaf out of the medieval book of heraldry too, so to speak. Their "heraldry" had clear associations with that of the Middle Ages, with its chivalrous significance, but was not by any means official. So the airmen were not restricted by any rules. They could choose any subject, form and colours they liked for their insignia, and could give free rein to their playfulness. And they certainly did, given the chance. The British pilots did not get the chance: the RFC, later RAF, frowned upon anything added to the official markings, which indeed sufficiently met the need for quick operational identification. But, beginning in 1916, aeroplanes of all the other belligerents (with the seeming exception of Turkey) were to be seen with all kinds of fanciful emblems, designs and colour schemes. Especially the Germans indulged in some most unusual paintwork and gaudy colours.

Also in 1916, the camouflaging of aeroplanes began to be undertaken systematically. It is interesting to note that in the conflict between the requirements of camouflage and the wish for showy markings the latter mostly won the day. An extreme — and well-publicized — example of this is that bright red was the main colour in which the aeroplanes of Manfred von Richthofen's *Geschwader* were painted. He himself (the "Red Baron") flew fighters that were finished in red,[3] while the other pilots had part of their planes painted in some other, distinguishing colour. The Allied pilots nicknamed his *Geschwader* and other units with such conspicuously painted aeroplanes "circuses", because their appearance was so much like that of a group of gaudily coloured circus caravans.

In what way and to what extent were the 20th-century aircraft markings associated with heraldry, and through this with the chivalric tradition?

As has been pointed out, there was no official connection, as the frequent use of unit markings in the form of a shield* might suggest. These were not genuinely heraldic. Yet, the choice of the form of a coat of arms reveals a wish to model the insignia upon the heraldic device which had its origins in chivalrous times.

This wish may be seen as one more desire on the part of

* Especially in the Second World War, by the Germans; less often in the First World War.

157

A pilot of 112 Sqn RAF posing by the nose of a Curtiss P-40 Kittyhawk with an impressive sharkmouth painted on the cowling. *(IWM)*

many airmen to emulate the medieval knights. And if, as was mostly the case, the shape of a coat of arms was not chosen, so that there was no evident link with heraldry, the various emblems and paint schemes with which the aeroplanes were decorated still served the same "beyond the merely practical" purpose that medieval heraldry did. They satisfied the need of being recognized — by friend and foe — as an individual warrior of some renown, or as one belonging to a famous and successful group. The visible expression of the pilots' pride of martial prowess and achievement — their bravado, if you will — no doubt bolstered their morale. In this light we must also see the custom for pilots and other aircrew to have a small mark painted on their aircraft for each aerial victory, each ship sunk, tank destroyed, etc., or each mission accomplished. This custom, which originated in the Second World War, produced some quite impressive "score-boards".

It is just possible that aircraft markings were sometimes deliberately put on to have a discouraging effect on the enemy. If so, it is rather difficult to substantiate. If ever there were markings that can be supposed to have had the intention of frightening the enemy, they were the sharkmouths painted on the front parts of aircraft, a practice that started as early as 1916 and became very popular in the air forces of both sides in the Second World War and later wars.[4] It seems doubtful, however, whether any pilot ever really believed that they would intimidate an enemy. In all probability the sharkmouths and suchlike markings were simply expressions of playfulness, as were many decorations on the armour of medieval knights. These, too, however impressive, cannot actually have been meant to frighten an adversary, nor have often done so in combat.

Traditionally, a romantic aura has surrounded the relations between the medieval knights and their ladies. Our conception of the ideal knight includes that he bore some token from his lady's dress (often a sleeve) or a lock of her hair when he participated in a tournament, or went into battle or on a crusade. In some cases the relationship was made plain for all to see. We are told that Duke William IX of Acquitaine had the image of his mistress painted on his shield, saying that "it was his will to bear her in battle, as she had borne him in bed".[5] As a modern counterpart, practically the same was done — but not with exactly the same motivation, I am sure — by Major Richard I. Bong, who was, with 40 victories, America's highest-scoring fighter ace of the Second World War, or any war. He had a large photograph of his fiancée Marge, with her name, applied to the nose of his Lockheed P-38 Lightning, the twin-engined fighter he flew in the south-west Pacific.

In a chapter on special aircraft markings one cannot very well refrain from at least mentioning the frolicsome decorative emblems which appeared on US combat aircraft — mostly the bombers — in the Second World War and also in the Korean War. They were usually painted on the nose section of the aircraft, and practically always featured scantily clad voluptuous girls, their images reflecting the aircrafts' names, which were suggestive and on occasion ambiguous, though good puns, like *Dinah Might* and *Miss Behave*, were rare. This unofficial embellishment of American military aircraft was widespread in the Second World War, and was regarded as a great morale booster for the crews. It is a good example of the play element in action, but for the rest has nothing to do with our subject.

8

Argument and conclusions

WITH the advantage of hindsight one can say that the revival of chivalry with the beginning of the war in the air was not very surprising. As we have seen, the First World War[1] provided an ideal matrix for such a rebirth, especially in its first years. There was individual combat again at close quarters, as in the Middle Ages, between men who could be considered — and indeed often considered themselves — members of an international brotherhood, as the medieval knights were. At the time, however, nobody will have foreseen the revival of an ethic that in the Western world was associated with the Middle Ages and was consequently regarded as something of the distant past and long dead, except in legend.

In the wars of the 20th century chivalry had only a short life. There was already a definite decline towards 1918, and though it was then still strong enough to be carried over to the Second World War, this was the last war in which it was observed at all. Korea, Vietnam and the wars in the Middle East — to mention only the most important later conflicts — saw none of it.

Nor, one would venture to predict, will there ever be another revival of chivalry, *in war*. It is necessary to support this prediction with some facts and arguments.

By the time the aeroplane arrived on the war scene, in the second decade of the 20th century, warfare on land and sea had long outgrown the stage at which warriors met in single or small-scale combat, clearly recognizable as human beings. The wars had become contests between nations, in which largely mechanized armies and fleets were employed, mostly engaging each other from such a distance and/or with such weapons that the combatants did not even see the enemy, in any case did not come into real personal contact with their adversaries. Rare exceptions in this respect were fights that scouting cavalry units got into.

With the war in the air it was different, at first. The aeroplane opened up an entirely new element to fight in, and did so at a time when it was still a very primitive machine and an even more primitive weapon. Indeed, it was quite some time before aeroplanes were armed for air-to-air fighting. If the aeroplane had existed for a much longer time before it was first used in war, it would have been a far more advanced machine and weapon when it made its belligerent debut. But as it happened, the aeroplane, which was not even taken seriously by all military commanders at the beginning, was first sent up into the war skies in an underdeveloped state. The airmen who met their opponents in the air in those primitive aeroplanes could clearly see them in the open cockpits, could gesture to them, but not seriously threaten them, not having any effective weapons at their disposal. All this gave their encounters a decidedly personal touch and a playful quality, which would not have been so if their aircraft had been those of a few decades later, with enclosed cockpits, fast and well armed.

Actually it is very strange that the aeroplane, which in the next quarter of a century was to develop into the most important weapon of all, should have made such an unwarlike first appearance on the war scene. Anyway, its primitive beginnings gave chivalry a better chance of taking root. In different circumstances the other factors — single combat, between men belonging to a kind of brotherhood — might not have been strong enough to bring about the revival of chivalry.

Shortly after chivalry had become established again, the prevailing conditions gradually became less favourable to its continued existence, even in the First World War. But, frail as it was, it survived, and had not yet died out in the Second World War. After this war, however, it was definitely extinct. In the war in the air, combat had come to be characterized by the same mechanical impersonality as the fighting on land and sea had, much earlier in history. It is a condition that is inimical to chivalry.

Sophisticated, impersonal and in many cases inhuman arms have now rendered all three elements man has fought wars in — land, sea and air — totally unfit for another revival of chivalry. And if — Heaven forbid! — space should be the next element in which mankind would wage war, it is inconceivable that there would ever arise that remarkable combination of factors that was seminal to the rebirth of chivalry at the beginning of the 1914-1918 air war. It is possible that there would be single combat in space war — as is still the case in the air war — but there would be nothing primitive about the weapons used, hardly any chance of close personal contact, and too great a dependence on computers and other electronic and mechanical devices to have any human feeling of belonging to the same international brotherhood as the adversary.

In chapter 2 we have seen that medieval chivalry served as a basis for international law. When chivalry reappeared in the 20th-century air war, it was not of comparable importance. It had no decisive influence on legislation, and only a minor influence on rules of a lower order. Nor did it have any effect on the outcome of a war or any battle, or even on the general behaviour of the combatants. It was, however, of great importance in another way. To those who set great store by moral values like honour, courtesy and fairness, the revival of chivalry in modern times was a confirmation of their conviction that those qualities were not just imaginary values, fostered and idealized by legend, but very real ones. And although, regretfully, chivalry was soon ousted from war again, the victim of a deplorable dehumanizing process, its recent revival has nevertheless strengthened its place in the human experience. No longer is it necessary to turn to the Middle Ages for — often legendary — examples of chivalry in war. They are now nearer at hand and more substantial, and they could move a man to live by chivalry's precepts in ordinary, peacetime life, as a gentleman.[2]

The advisability of describing the short-lived chivalry in the 20th-century air war as faithfully as possible will be clear. History should take the matter in hand, before legend lays too strong a hold on it.

Before we close this book, there is one last important subject that must be dealt with. There is a danger that one is so much carried away by one's enthusiasm for the ideal of chivalry, the grand style and in particular the notion of war as a noble game of honour, that one is led to idealize and praise war, even comes to see war as the origin of many human virtues and accomplishments. This extreme view was held, for instance, by John Ruskin, the 19th-century English critic and essayist, who said that he found

> that all the great nations learned the truth of word, and strength of thought, in war; that they were nourished in war, and wasted by peace — in a word, that they were born in war, and expired in peace.[3]

Ruskin concedes that this is not true of *every* war. In his opinion the ideal of "creative or foundational" war was realized in Sparta and in medieval chivalry. And we must remember that he did not live to see the horrors of the two world wars in our century. Still, such extravagant utterances are not conducive to a balanced judgement on the effects of war — good and bad — on mankind, or on the value of chivalry.

Chivalry does not need exaggerated support and praise. The true facts — objectively stated — bear out the beneficial influence it has had on warfare, and its potential to raise the tone of society.

Notes

Chapter 1

1. The encounter with Guynemer is described by Udet in his
   autobiography *Mein Fliegerleben* (1935) on pages 58-60. The
   (translated) quotation is from this book. The exact date of the
   event could not be traced. It must have been before 19 June, the
   day Gontermann came back from leave, taking over the
   command of *Jasta 15* from Udet, who had been in temporary
   command, a take-over that Udet in his book places after the fight
   with Guynemer.

   I have not been able to determine whether Udet flew an
   Albatros D III or D V. The D V did not reach the front until May
   1917. Both types had wing failure problems, though. It is
   practically certain that Guynemer flew a SPAD with the new 180
   hp Hispano-Suiza 8Ab engine. It is known that Guynemer was
   allotted the first example of this new version, which was first
   delivered in the spring of 1917. Anyway, even the SPAD with the
   150 hp Hispano-Suiza was superior to both the Albatros D III
   and D V, a fact that had become painfully apparent to the
   German pilots at the front.

   Udet thought at the time that Guynemer had shot down 30
   German aircraft. Actually the Frenchman's score then stood at
   45 (only surpassed by Manfred von Richthofen, whose score was
   then 52).

2. Understandably, there are not many cases on record in which a
   pilot or crew of an aeroplane surrendered in the air. Not that it
   was in itself impracticable to indicate that one wanted to give up
   the fight. In the First World War the pilot or observer/gunner,
   flying in open cockpits, could do this by holding up his hands. In

the Second World War, when most aircraft had a retractable undercarriage, this could be lowered, which was generally accepted as a sign of surrender. Also, it is conceivable that the crew could surrender by showing a white cloth of some sort. But to make the intention to surrender clear enough to the enemy to keep him from pressing his attack was quite another matter in the fire and fury of a fight, with occasionally more than one enemy aircraft involved, everyone flying at great speeds, especially in World War II. And even if successful in this, there was for the victor the difficulty of accepting the surrender, which was only feasible when the pilot who surrendered was over or not too far from his enemy's territory, so that the victorious aircraft could "shepherd" his adversary to an airfield or other place where he could land and where others could take the crew prisoner and impound the machine.

3. Lord French, *1914* (1919), p.340. The words "some such" refer to an exchange of courtesies between himself and an enemy general in the Boer War, which he had just told about.

4. H. B. Swope, *Inside the German Empire* (1917), p.185.

5. E. Alexander Powell, *Vive la France* (1916), p.212.

6. Admiral Mark Kerr, *Land, Sea and Air* (1927), p.286.

7. W. M. Fry, *Air of Battle* (1974), p.124.

8. Thomas R. Funderburk, *The Fighters; The Men and Machines of the First Air War* (1965), p.67.

9. Albert Ball and Werner Voss were aces (that is, had shot down five or more enemy aeroplanes) before they were 20 years old!

10. Henry Bordeaux, *Vie héroique de Guynemer* (1918).

11. G. V. Williams, *With our Army in Flanders* (1915), p.332.

12. J. M. Spaight, *Air Power and War Rights* (3rd ed., 1947), p.110.

13. On 22 November 1973 *Jagdgeschwader 74* of the Federal Republic of Germany's Luftwaffe was given the name of Werner Mölders, an early ace in the Second World War. He was killed in a flying accident on 22 November 1941. The present Luftwaffe also still honours three German aces of the First World War, by naming units after them: Richthofen, Boelcke and Immelmann.

14. Quoted in Christopher Shores & Hans Ring, *Fighters over the Desert* (1969), p.223.

15. Edward H. Sims, *Fighter Tactics and Strategy 1914-1970* (1972), p.175. Major Erich Rudorffer, who was one of the deadliest marksmen in the Luftwaffe, ended the war as Germany's seventh-ranking ace, with 222 victories to his credit. The remarkable thing about his victory tally is that it is so varied. Having fought on all three of Germany's fronts during the war — in the West, in North Africa and on the Russian front — he had

shot down just about every type the Allies used against the Luftwaffe. In the last few months of the war Rudorffer flew the Messerschmitt Me 262 jet fighter, in which he won his last 12 victories. He was awarded the Oak Leaves and Swords to the Knight's Cross.

Chapter 2

1. For those who want to know more about this subject, scholarly works are readily available, e.g. Maurice Keen, *Chivalry* (1984).
2. Huizinga's study was first published (in Dutch) in 1938. I have used an English translation (© 1950, by Roy Publishers), reprinted as a paperback by Beacon Press, Boston, by arrangement with Routledge & Kegan Paul, Ltd, London.
3. Huizinga, *op.cit.*, p.89.
4. Huizinga, *op. cit.*, pp.89-90. The words "lesser breeds without the Law" are from Rudyard Kipling's poem *Recessional*.
5. Huizinga, *op. cit.*, p.90.
6. Sholto Douglas, *Years of Combat* (1963), p.40. The quote within the quote is from the soldier poet Edmund Blunden (1896-1974).
7. Sydney Painter, *French Chivalry* (1940), p.54.
8. Maurice Keen, *Chivalry* (1984), p.101.
9. Huizinga, *op. cit.*, pp.96, 104 & 180.
10. President Roosevelt addressed Congress in the early afternoon of 8 December 1941, reporting the events at Pearl Harbor and asking that Congress declare a state of war with Japan. His opening words were: "Yesterday, December 7, 1941 — a date which will live in infamy — the United States of America was suddenly and deliberately attacked . . .".
11. V. Hardesty, *Red Phoenix; The Rise of Soviet Air Power 1941-1945.* (1982), pp.130-1.
12. Ibid., p.141.
13. Werner Girbig, *Jagdgeschwader 5 "Eismeerjäger"* (1975), p.221.
14. Hardesty, *op. cit.*, pp.121 ff.

Chapter 3

1. Charles A. Lindbergh (1902-1974) was a civilian in World War II. He had for a short time been a colonel in the Army Air Corps, but, feeling gravely insulted by President Roosevelt, tendered his resignation on 28 April 1941. He performed valuable war service for his country, however, as a test pilot and an aviation consultant. In 1944 he spent five months in the Pacific with the Navy and the Marine Corps as an adviser on fighter planes. Flying with fighter pilots on combat missions he did not restrict

his activities to observing combat, but also fired his guns in anger and dive-bombed enemy positions. Once, on 28 July 1944, he even shot down a Japanese fighter off the south coast of Ceram. As he had no combatant status, he thereby violated international law. When, more than once, commanders expressed concern about this, warning that if the Japanese captured him he would be shot, Lindbergh replied that "he didn't see it made much difference what status you were on if you were forced down on Jap territory, because according to reports they shot you anyway". (*The Wartime Journals of Charles A. Lindbergh*, 1970, p.818).

2. *The Wartime Journals of Charles A. Lindbergh* (1970), p.821.
3. It is curious, by the way, that before the aeroplane was actually used in war some people thought that ramming would be the usual method of attacking enemy planes. Clément Ader (1841-1925), a French aviation pioneer, contemplated a kind of 'cavalry charge' in the air, after which the side that went in with the greater number would be left with air superiority! (Clément Ader, *l'Aviation Militaire*, 1909).
4. J. M. Spaight, *Air Power and War Rights* (3rd ed., 1947), p.156.
5. I have not succeeded in finding out when the Germans first made parachutes available to their pilots. The earliest case I have found in which a parachute saved a pilot's life was when in July or August 1917 the German ace Paul W. Bäumer of *Jasta 5*, shortly after shooting down a Bristol fighter (his 30th victory) had to bale out of his Albatros fighter, which had been set on fire by another Bristol fighter. He came down unhurt. Bäumer has described this incident in his contribution to Werner von Langsdorff, *Flieger am Feind* (1935), pp.173-5.

   The Allies did not see fit to provide their pilots and (aeroplane) observers with parachutes in World War I, though it would have been possible to do so, even earlier than the Germans did: a disgraceful policy.
6. World War I was not the first war in which observation balloons were used. As early as 2 June 1794 the French Revolutionary forces used one (called *l'Entreprenant*) at Maubeuge, which was then being bombarded by Dutch and Austrian troops. The enemy officers regarded aerial observation as an unsporting breach of the rules of gentlemanly warfare! Observation balloons were also used in the American Civil War (1861-65), the Franco-Prussian War of 1870-1, the Boer War (1899-1902) and in several other, minor, conflicts, without the benefit of parachutes, however. (Donald Dale Jackson, *The Aeronauts* (1981), pp.75 ff.).

7. In a great storm on 5 May 1916, no fewer than 24 French balloons broke loose from their cables near Verdun and a number of them were driven over the German lines. The observers escaped for the most part by parachute. See Spaight, *Air Power and War Rights* (3rd ed., 1947), pp.155-6. In a footnote a few more cases are mentioned in which a balloon was torn from its moorings by a gale or its cable was cut by enemy artillery fire.

8. Ira ("Taffy") Jones, *Tiger Squadron. The Story of 74 Squadron R.A.F. in Two World Wars.* (1954), p.24.

9. Ibid., p.115.

10. Ibid., p.130.

11. From the English translation (*The German Air Force in the Great War*; 1920), quoted in John Lucas, *The Big Umbrella* (1973), p.57.

12. In his *Histoire Illustrée de la Guerre aérienne* (1920), pp.284-6.

13. Douglas Reed, *Insanity Fair* (1938).

14. Sholto Douglas, in the first volume of his autobiography, *Years of Combat* (1963), on p.201, calls the powerful hatred for the Germans which Mannock had developed unaccountable; "most of us had no great feeling of animosity: they were the enemy that we had to cope with, but hatred of them in an emotional sense, was a rare thing". MacLanachan ('McScotch'), Mannock's friend in 40 Sqn, makes a distinction: "to the Germans as individuals he showed an extreme consideration and admiration as strong in the one direction as was his hatred for the organisation for which they were fighting in the other." ('McScotch', *Fighter Pilot*, 1936, p.245). This would be borne out by the entry in Mannock's diary for 19 August 1917 in which he described "a splendid fight" he had had on 12 August with *Leutnant* Joachim von Bertrab. The German was wounded and had to land. "I was very pleased I did not kill him," Mannock wrote. (Frederick Oughton & Vernon Smyth, *Ace with One Eye*, 1963, p.182).

On the other hand, Major K. L. Caldwell, Mannock's Commanding Officer in 74 Sqn, has described a vicious attack that he made on a German two-seater which had crashed, but not badly, within the Allied lines: "He dived half-a-dozen times at the machine, spraying bullets at the pilot and the observer, who were still showing signs of life. [. . .] On being questioned as to his wild behaviour after we had landed, he heatedly replied, 'The swines are better dead — no prisoners for me!'" (Quoted in Oughton & Smyth, *op. cit.*, p.259). The memory of this ugly scene did not, however, keep Keith L. Caldwell (who had risen to the rank of Air Commodore, RNZAF) from writing in a foreword to a later biography of Mannock: "Mick was a very human, sensitive sort of chap; he did not hate people or things at all. He has, however, gained the reputation of being a fervent 'Hun-hater'. I believe that this hatred was calculated or assumed to boost his own morale and that of the squadron in general. This was the sort of war-going outlook it rather paid to have." (James M. Dudgeon, *'Mick'; The Story of Major Edward Mannock, VC, DSO, MC,* 1981).

It seems unlikely that we shall ever know Mannock's true attitude towards his enemies.

15. Capt. J. E. Doyle, DFC (60 Sqn), quoted in Alan Morris, *The Balloonatics* (1970), p.157.
16. Alan Morris, *The Balloonatics* (1970), p.86.
17. Capt. A. C. Reid, *'Planes and Personalities* (1920), p.134.
18. W. A. Wellman, *Go, Get'Em* (1918), p.234.
19. Morris, *op. cit.*, p.85.
20. F. M. Cutlack, *The Australian Flying Corps* (Vol. VIII of the *Official History of Australia in the War*) (1923), p.284.
21. J. N. Hall, *High Adventure* (1918), p.146.
22. Quoted in Morris, *op, cit.*, p.86.
23. Morris, *op. cit.*, p.86.
24. After Frank Luke's death, only Eddie Rickenbacker surpassed Luke's tally, to become America's top-ranking ace in the First World War. Luke was also the first American airman to win his country's highest award, the Congressional Medal of Honor. Although awarded posthumously, his was the only one to be awarded to an airman during the course of the war. Seven other airmen, among them Eddie Rickenbacker, were given the decoration, but only after years of consideration.
25. See Norman S. Hall, *The Balloon Buster; Frank Luke of Arizona* (1928), pp.95-102. Also Arch Whitehouse, *The Years of the Sky Kings* (1959), pp.280-1, and Alan Morris, *op. cit.*, p.173.
26. Arch Whitehouse, *The Years of the Sky Kings* (1959), p.274.
27. See J. M. Spaight, *Air Power and War Rights* (3rd ed., 1947), which also comprises the complete Air Warfare Rules 1923, in an appendix.
28. L. S. Larrazábal, *La guerra de Espana desde el aire* (1969). I have used the German translation *Das Flugzeug im Spanischen Bürgerkrieg* (1973), in which this incident is mentioned on p.425.
29. José Ruiz Gómez was killed on 25 June 1938.
30. Francísco Tarazona Torán, *Sangre en el cielo* (n.d.), quoted by Larrazábal on p.467 (of the German translation).
31. Larrazábal, *op. cit*, p.442 (of the German translation).
32. The *idea* to use parachute troops was by no means new. In October 1918, General John J. Pershing, commander-in-chief of

the US forces in France, gave his tentative approval to an ambitious (in fact quite unrealistic) plan by Colonel William Mitchell to drop 12,000 soldiers behind the German lines in the Metz sector, using bombers as troop carriers, each carrying ten men, not counting the two-man crew. The operation was to have been carried out in the spring of 1919. (Isaac Don Levine, *Mitchell: Pioneer of Air Power* (1943), pp. 146-51.)

In a sense, the Russians pioneered the use of paratroops. They experimented with them during their manoeuvres in the 1930s, with a climax in 1936, when, during the summer manoeuvres in the Ukraine, they astonished the foreign military observers with a simultaneous drop of 1000 paratroopers, who prepared the terrain for 5000 airborne troops that followed them. But, strangely enough, the Russians made only limited use of paratroops in actual war. The Germans, however, who had been quick to adopt the idea and had created their first paratroop battalion as early as 1935, used their *Fallschirmjäger* on a large scale and very effectively in World War II, as did the British and Americans later in the war. The Japanese also employed paratroops, but on a small scale.

33. Raymond F. Toliver & Trevor J. Constable, *Fighter Aces of the Luftwaffe* (1977), p.21. The first edition of this book was published in 1968 under the title *Horrido!*.

34. In his description of the incident on page 378 of his book, Townsend says the RAF pilot was Sergeant J. H. Dickinson, who was a member of 253 Sqn, too. This is probably an error. Sergeant Dickinson was also shot down on 30 August, also baled out, and was also dead when he landed. But what caused his death is not clear. If he had also been gunned to death while going down in his parachute, as P/O Jenkins certainly was, it is highly unlikely that Townsend would not have mentioned two such killings of members of the same squadron on the same day. For the relevant data, see Winston G. Ramsey (Ed.), *The Battle of Britain Then and Now.* (1980), p.394.

35. J. A. Kent, *One of the Few* (1971), p.120.

36. Quoted in Winston G. Ramsay (Ed.), *The Battle of Britain Then and Now* (1980), p.453.

37. Peter Townsend, *Duel of Eagles* (1970), p.288.

38. Ramsey, *op. cit.*, p.453.

39. Adolf Galland, *Die Ersten und die Letzten* (1953), p.135. An English translation of this book was published in 1954, under the title *The First and the Last*.

40. Ibid., pp.135-6.

41. C. F. Rawnsley & Robert Wright, *Night Fighter* (1957), p.28.

42. Toliver & Constable, *op. cit.*, p.376, footnote.

43. Galland, *op. cit.*, p.375.

44. See, for instance: Walther Dahl, *Rammjäger* (1961), pp.119-20. Edward H. Sims, *Fighter Tactics and Strategy 1914-1970* (1972), p.175. Werner Girbig, *Start im Morgengrauen* (1973), p.38 & p.74. Helmut Lipfert, *Das Tagebuch des Hauptmann Lipfert* (1973), p.241.

45. Jeffrey Ethell & Alfred Price, *The German Jets in Combat* (1979), pp.33-4.

46. The first Allied crew who met an Me 262 fighter and came home to tell the tale, were Flight-Lieutenant A. E. Wall and his observer (544 Photo Reconnaissance Sqn, RAF). On 25 July 1944 their unarmed De Havilland Mosquito was attacked by an Me 262 at 29,000 ft near Munich. Wall succeeded in out-manoeuvring the jet fighter, and they escaped to their base in Italy without suffering any hits. Before that, two USAAF Lockheed Lightnings and one RAF Mosquito had been shot down by Me 262s of *Erprobungskommando 262*, which, from late June, had performed experimental interceptions of high-flying Allied photo-reconnaissance aircraft. (William Green, *The Warplanes of the Third Reich* (1970), p.634).

47. Walther Dahl, *Rammjäger* (1961), p.136.

48. Richard E. Turner, *Mustang Pilot* (1969), p.61.

49. Ibid., p.115.

50. Lord James Douglas-Hamilton (Ed.), *The Air Battle for Malta; The Diaries of a Fighter Pilot*. (1981), pp.17-18.

51. Jack Currie, *Lancaster Target* (1977), p.159.

52. Quoted in Christopher Shores, Hans Ring & William N. Hess, *Fighters over Tunisia* (1975), p.394.

53. J. R. D. "Bob" Braham, *"Scramble!"* (1961), pp.193-4. In fact, two of the German crew (of 3) got clear of the Bf 110 and went down by parachute. One of them drowned, the other was picked up by a Dornier Do 18, after 18 hours in the water. (Ab A. Jansen, *Wespennest Leeuwarden II* (1976), p.308.

54. *The Wartime Journals of Charles A. Lindbergh* (1970), p.857.

55. Robert Sherrod, *History of Marine Corps Aviation in World War II* (1952), p.140.

56. In some cases the Soviets tried to induce the captured men to change sides, to fight with them against the fascists. A few Germans gratefully availed themselves of this opportunity to return to their side of the lines. For obvious reasons they were then posted away from the Russian front. See: Werner Girbig, *Jagdgeschwader 5 "Eismeerjäger"* (1975), pp.100, 106, 120, 157 & 202.

57. Bruce Robertson (Ed.), *Air Aces of the 1914-1918 War* (1959), pp.64-5.
58. Eddie V. Rickenbacker, *Fighting the Flying Circus* (1919), p.268.
59. 'McScotch' (pseudonym of MacLanachan), *Fighter Pilot* (1936), pp.110-12.
60. The same sentiment was expressed by Joseph Conrad, when, writing of the Royal Navy in Nelson's time, he wrote: "It was a fortunate navy. Its victories were no mere smashing of helpless ships and massacres of cowed men. It was spared that cruel favour, for which no brave heart had ever prayed. It was fortunate in its adversaries. I say adversaries, for on recalling such proud memories we should avoid the word "enemies", whose hostile sound perpetuates the antagonisms and strife of nations so irremediable perhaps, so fateful — and also so vain." (*The Mirror of the Sea* (1906), p.192 of Dent's Collected Edition).
61. Galland, *op. cit.*, pp.66-7. In his book Galland states that the Hurricanes were Belgian. Only years later did he find out that they were RAF fighters.
62. Alan Morris, *The Balloonatics* (1970), p.119. This book gives a detailed account of the "von Eschwege" incident, upon which I have freely drawn.
63. W. Arthur Bishop, *The Courage of the Early Morning* (1965), pp.57-8.
64. Morris, *op. cit.*, pp.173-4.
65. Thomas R. Funderburk, *The Fighters; The Men and Machines of the First Air War* (1965), p.67.

Chapter 4

1. This German decoration could be regarded as about the equivalent of the Victoria Cross or Congressional Medal of Honor. Originally it was a Prussian order, and it had a French name because the French language was used by preference at the Prussian court, especially when Frederick the Great — a great admirer of French culture — became king in 1740. That same year he changed the name of an existing order *(Ordre Pour la Générosité)* into *Ordre Pour le Mérite*. The decoration was a blue Maltese cross, with the words *Pour/le Mé/rite* on the two horizontal arms and the lower vertical one, and a crowned 'F' on the upper vertical arm. It was nicknamed *Der Blaue Max* (The Blue Max). No one seems to know why. The German ace *Leutnant* Carl Degelow (the very last winner of the *Pour le Mérite*) writes in his memoirs:

It is said that when [Max] Immelmann's *Pour le Mérite* was fastened around his neck, the blue enamel of the actual medal cast a reflection on his otherwise pale countenance and, from that time forward, the decoration became known as 'the Blue Max'. (English translation, Kimber 1979, p.36).

Somehow this explanation is not very convincing. It is an interesting speculation that the name Max might be made up of 'Ma' for Maltese and 'x' for cross.

The First World War was the last in which the *Pour le Mérite* was awarded, but recipients still wore it in World War II, Göring, Udet and Osterkamp being notable examples among airmen.

2. This was Fok.F I 103/17. Voss first flew it on 29 August. The other pre-production machine, Fok.F I 102/17, was reserved for von Richthofen himself, who flew it for the first time on 1 September. (A. R. Weyl, *Fokker: The Creative Years* (1965), pp.231-2.).

3. Bruce Robertson (Ed.), *Von Richthofen and the Flying Circus* (1958), p.79.

4. James Byford McCudden, *Flying Fury* (1930), p.186. (This book was originally published in 1918 under the title of *Five Years in the Royal Flying Corps*.).

5. Ibid., p.187.

6. A detailed account of Voss's last fight is given in Christopher Cole, *McCudden V.C.* (1967), pp.119-21.

7. Arthur Rhys Davids was killed in action a month later, on 27 October 1917. A few weeks before his death he had received the D.S.O. In a dinner speech he gave on that occasion he said

that he was very much honoured to receive the D.S.O., and was very pleased indeed, but he would very much like to express his appreciation of the enemy whom we had daily fought, and who as a rule put up such fine examples of bravery and courage, and he felt that he was perhaps doing an unprecedented thing when he asked us all to rise to drink to "Von Richthofen, our most worthy enemy", which toast we all drank with the exception of one non-flying officer who remained seated, and said, "No, I won't drink to the health of that devil." (McCudden, *op. cit.*, p.196).

It is significant that the only one who refused to drink the proposed toast was a *non*-flying officer. He did not belong to the international brotherhood of airmen; he would not understand the affinity that existed between them even if they fought on different sides.

8. McCudden, *op. cit.*, p.187.

9. J. M. Spaight, *Air Power and War Rights* (3rd ed., 1947), in footnotes on pp.349-52, gives a great number of instances of

burials of enemy airmen with military honours.

10. Floyd Gibbons, *The Red Knight of Germany* (1927), pp.368-9.

11. Kenneth Poolman, *Zeppelins over England* (1960), p.173.

12. *The Aeroplane*, 13 September 1916 and Ernst Lehmann, *Auf Luftpatrouille und Weltfahrt* (1930), p.166.

13. House of Commons Debates, vol. 390, col. 386.

14. Alan Morris, *The Balloonatics* (1970), p.120.

15. H. A. Jones, *Over the Balkans and South Russia* (1923), p.94.

16. Ibid., pp.87-8.

17. Manfred Freiherr von Richthofen, *Der Rote Kampfflieger* (1933), p.116. (This book, first published in 1917, was translated into English under the title *The Red Air Fighter*.).

18. Lieutenant-Colonel Tyrrel Mann Hawker, MC, *Hawker, V.C.* (1965), p.240.

19. In Bruce Robertson (Ed.), *Von Richthofen and the Flying Circus* (1958) there is, on page 30, a photograph showing Boelcke and von Richthofen talking to *Leutnant* Otto Höhne seated in the cockpit of a captured DH2. This photograph was taken in September 1916.

20. Gibbons, *op. cit.*, p.100.

21. Hawker, *op. cit.*, p.237 (footnote).

22. Gibbons, *op. cit.*, p.100.

23. Hawker, *op. cit.*, p.245.

24. For example, B. A. Molter, *Knights of the Air* (1918), pp.21-4, and Henry Serrano Villard, *Contact! The Story of the Early Birds* (1968), p.234.

25. Villard, *op. cit.*, p.194.

26. Charles Harvard Gibbs-Smith, *Aviation: An Historical Survey.* (1970), p.166, footnote 3.

27. Thomas R. Funderburk, *The Fighters; The Men and Machines of the First Air War.* (1965, 1966), p.33.

28. M. Mortane, *La Guerre aérienne,* 7 November 1918, p.835. There is a photograph of the wreath in Bonnefon, *Le Premier 'As' Pégoud* (1918), p.128.

29. Charles Dollfus, Henry Beaubois & Camille Rougeron, *l'Homme, l'Air et l'Espace* (1965), p.185, where it is stated that the ribbon attached to the wreath is kept in the *Musee de l'Armée aux Invalides* in Paris. In Mahlke, *Hoch in den Lüften* (1916) the same French text on the ribbon is mentioned, on p.112.

30. A. R. Weyl, *Fokker: The Creative Years* (1965), p.106.

31. Ibid., p.106.

32. *Immelmann, "Der Adler von Lille"* (Edited by his brother Franz) (1934), p.102. (An English translation, under the title *Immelmann, The Eagle of Lille*, was published in 1959).

33. Quoted in Prof. Dr Johannes Werner, *Boelcke, der Mensch, der Flieger, der Führer der deutschen Jagdfliegerei* (1932), p.109. (An English translation, under the title *Knight of Germany*, was published in 1933.) Shortly before Immelmann's victory Boelcke had missed a good chance of being the first to shoot down an enemy aircraft in a Fokker monoplane, because his gun jammed. But he certainly did not grudge Immelmann his success, and wrote that he had made a fine and dashing job of it.

34. *Immelmann, "Der Adler von Lille"*, p.104.

35. Rudolf Oskar Gottschalk, *Boelcke† Deutschlands Fliegerheld* (1916), p.39.

36. Gottschalk, *op. cit.*, p.45, Immelmann, *op. cit.*, pp.146 & 153, and Werner, *op. cit.*, p.187.

37. The Immelmann turn is often described incorrectly as "a half loop, ending with a roll-out at the top". I quote the following accurate description from J. E. Johnson, *Full Circle: The Story of Air Fighting* (1964), p.18:

> The German pilot's manoeuvre, known for long afterwards as 'the Immelmann turn', began with a dive upon his enemy. After building up his speed in the dive he pulled the Fokker into a climb and opened fire from behind and below to gain surprise. After firing he continued climbing, as if he were going to loop, but when his Fokker reached a vertical position he kicked on hard rudder, turned sideways and dived on his opponent from the opposite direction. The German dived, fired, 'Immelmanned', and attacked again, and the tactic was sound so long as the Fokker was superior to all other machines on the Western Front. The Immelmann turn was very successful because the aggressor quickly regained his height and could attack again and again. But later, when more powerful engines became available, it was a dangerous move, for the lower pilot could climb after the Fokker and attack when it hung almost motionless in the vertical position, not under full control, and presenting an easy shot.

38. Norman L. R. Franks, *Max Immelmann — "Eagle of Lille"*.(*Air Pictorial*, June 1974).

39. Immelmann, *op. cit.*, p.184.

40. Franks, *op.cit.*

41. Gerald Rawling, in an interesting article in *Air Pictorial* (September 1973 issue), *Air Aces of World War I. Who was the greatest of them all?*, applies victory score, personal bravery and leadership as criteria, but not chivalry. His final ranking (1. Mannock, 2. von Richthofen, 3. McCudden and 4. Boelcke) therefore differs from what mine would be. With the data at my disposal I would rate Boelcke as the greatest.

42. The rules are quoted in Werner, *op. cit.*, p.168.
43. Werner, *op. cit.*, p.168.
44. Werner, *op. cit.*, p.188.
45. Funderburk, *op. cit.*, p.78.
46. Gottschalk, *op. cit.*, p.40.
47. Werner, *op. cit.*, pp.127-8.
48. Hawker, *op. cit.*, pp.221-2.
49. Prof. Dr Johannes Werner (Ed.), *Briefe eines deutschen Kampffliegers an ein junges Mädchen* (1930), p.73. In an earlier letter Erwin Böhme describes Boelcke's last flight. (pp.69-71).
50. Particulars of the ceremonies in Cambrai, the train journey and the funeral in Dessau are to be found in Werner, *Boelcke* (1932), pp.210-14 and in Gottschalk, *op. cit.*, pp.91-7.
51. In Werner, *Boelcke* (1932) there is, opposite p.193, a photograph of the note. Notice the misspelled name.
52. Werner, *Briefe eines deutschen Kampffliegers* (1930), p.171.
53. Denis Richards, *Royal Air Force 1939-1945 Vol. I The Fight at Odds* (1953), p.243.

Chapter 5

1. Duncan Grinnell-Milne, *Wind in the Wires* (1933), pp.124-5 (of the 1968 Doubleday reissue).
2. Chaz Bowyer, *Albert Ball, V.C.* (1977), p.97.
3. W. M. Fry, *Air of Battle* (1974), p.79.
4. Edwin C. Parsons, *I Flew with the Lafayette Escadrille* (1937, 1963), p.79.
5. Herbert Molloy Mason, Jr. *The Lafayette Escadrille* (1964), p.130.
6. *Coastal Command.* The Air Ministry Account of the Part Played by Coastal Command in the Battle of the Seas 1939-1942 (1942), p.50.
7. Mortane, *Les Vols émouvants de la Guerre* (1917), p.20.
8. J. M. Spaight, *Air Power and War Rights* (3rd ed., 1947), p.352, (footnote 5).
9. F. M. Cutlack, *The Australian Flying Corps* (1923), p.58.
10. Alan Morris, *First of the Many; The Story of Independent Force, RAF* (1968), p.55.
11. Quoted in *La Guerre aérienne*, 22 May 1918, p.455.
12. Cutlack, *op. cit.*, p.72.
13. C. J. Biddle, *The Way of the Eagle* (1919), p.243.
14. A. Ritter von Tutschek, *Stürme und Luftsiege* (1918), pp.158-9.
15. *La Guerre aérienne*, 10 May 1917, p.410; quoted in Spaight, *op.*

cit., pp.354-5. There is a discrepancy here. According to Bruce Robertson (Ed.), *Air Aces of the 1914-1918 War* (1959), p.127, Olivari did not score the first of his 12 victories until 23 August 1917.

16. Quoted in *Flight,* 13 April 1916.
17. Hans Schröder, *Erlebter Krieg* (ca.1934), p.163.
18. Letter quoted in *La Guerre aérienne*, 14 June 1917, p.485.
19. Wedgwood Benn, *In the Side Shows* (1919), p.247. Quoted in Spaight, *op. cit.*, p.355.
20. Capt. A. C. Reid, *'Planes and Personalities* (1920), p.139.
21. Cutlack, *op. cit.*, p.72.
22. H. A. Jones, *Over the Balkans and South Russia* (1923), p.33.
23. Mason, *op. cit.*, pp.242-3.
24. Parsons, *op. cit.*, pp.306-7.
25. Cutlack, *op. cit.*, p.58.
26. This flight of the imagination brings to mind the humorous story Edwin Parsons has told about what happened when, one day in September 1917, a German observation plane out of fuel landed on their airfield. While his *Unteroffizier* observer sat silent in his cockpit,

    the extremely snooty officer pilot refused to surrender or talk to anyone except the highest-ranking officer on the field.
        When the commandant arrived, the German naïvely asked to be serviced up and allowed to go on his way; mentioned that aviation was a sporting game and we should play it like sportsmen; said he'd do the same for any Allied aviator in distress.
        The German was indignant when the commandant quietly and politely explained that, owing to the fact that there was a war on, he was unable to grant the request, reasonable as it seemed.
        Then the Boche made another proposition: If we would furnish him the gas so that he could get into the air, we could send any plane we chose up after him and he'd take the chance of battling his way back to the lines. But he insisted on fair play. Five minutes' start and only one plane to come in pursuit.
        Of course, he got the horse cackle from everyone and was taken away, sadly shaking his head over the unsportsmanlike conduct of his enemies.

    (Parsons, *op. cit.*, pp.304-5).
27. Bernard Pares, *Day by Day with the Russian Army* (1915), pp.168-71.
28. Spaight, *op. cit.*, p.113.
29. Schütz, in Neumann, *Die deutschen Luftstreitkräfte im Weltkriege* (1920), pp.540-3.
30. Lieutenant-Colonel J. E. Tennant, *In the Clouds above Baghdad*, p.49.

31. Parsons, *op. cit.*, pp.251-2.
32. Mason, *op. cit.*, pp.10, 42-3, 90 (footnote), 119-20, 161, 289.
33. Schäfer, *Vom Jäger zum Flieger* (1918), p.97.
34. Quoted in James J. Hudson, *Hostile Skies; A Combat History of the American Air Service in World War I* (1968), p.129.
35. Spaight, *op. cit.*, p.117.
36. Ibid., p.117.
37. James Ambrose Brown, *A Gathering of Eagles.* (Vol.II of *South African Forces World War II*) (1970), p.275.
38. Ibid., p.275.
39. *L'Aeronautica Italiana nella Seconda Guerra Mondiale*, vol. 2, p.186.
40. Brown, *op. cit.*, p.276.
41. R. Leslie Oliver, *Malta Besieged* (1944), p.30.
42. For the same reason pilots who described their war experiences in books published during the war often used a pseudonym, and did not reveal the names of their comrades or the number of their unit, either. For example, in 1917 a book called *Cavalry of the Clouds* came out, under the pen-name "Contact". The author was Captain Alan Bott, who dedicated his book "to the Fallen of Umpty Squadron, R.F.C.", which was 70 Sqn. When Paul Richey's personal record of the campaign in France was published in 1941, under the title *Fighter Pilot*, no name of the author was mentioned, not even a pen-name. Ronald Adam, an RAF controller and ex RFC flyer, used the pseudonym "Blake" when he wrote his books *Readiness at Dawn* (1941) and *We Rendezvous at Ten* (1942). He used the name "Bo'sun Spritt" for the famous Group Captain 'Sailor' Malan.
43. Raymond F. Toliver & Trevor J. Constable, *Fighter Aces of the Luftwaffe* (1977), p.220.
44. Hans Peter Hagen, *Husaren des Himmels* (1964), p.214. According to Hagen, the birthday greeting was broadcast by the BBC in London; Toliver and Constable say it was done by a military radio station at Calais, which seems more likely.
45. To be exact, the very highest German decoration was the *Gold Oak Leaves with Swords and Diamonds to the Knight's Cross*, instituted by Hitler on 29 December 1944. It was stipulated that it was not to be awarded more than 12 times. In fact the one and only man to receive the award was the famous Stuka pilot Hans-Ulrich Rudel, who was given it by the *Führer* on 1 January 1945.
46. Quoted by Norman L. R. Franks in his article *Max Immelmann —"Eagle of Lille"* (*Air Pictorial*, June 1974).
47. Bruce Robertson (Ed.), *Air Aces of the 1914-1918 War* (1959), p.82.

48. B. A. Molter, *Knights of the Air* (1918), pp.27-32.
49. Robertson, *op. cit.*, p.64.
50. Colin Hodgkinson, *Best Foot Forward* (1957), pp.162-3.
51. Toliver & Constable, *op. cit.*, p.257.
52. J. Huizinga, *Homo Ludens: A Study of the Play-Element in Culture.* (English translation, 1950) p.99.
53. Ernst Udet, *Mein Fliegerleben* (1935), caption of photograph after p.88.
54. J. M. Bruce, *The Fokker Dr.I* (Profile Publication No. 55, 1965).
55. J. M. Bruce, *The de Havilland DH4* (Profile Publication No. 26, 1965).

Chapter 6

1. Robert Mason, *Chickenhawk* (1983), p.393.
2. *Immelmann, "Der Adler von Lille"*, pp.124-5. Lieutenant Slade's letter was quoted in the *Daily Mail* of 10 April 1916.
3. Immelmann, *op. cit.*, pp.145-6.
4. J. M. Spaight, *Air Power and War Rights* (3rd ed., 1947), p.114 (Quoting from Mortane, *Histoire illustrée de la Guerre aérienne*, 1920, I.73).
5. Armand van Ishoven, *The Fall of an Eagle: The Life of Fighter Ace Ernest Udet.* (© 1977; English version by Chaz Bowyer, 1979), pp.36-7.
6. Ibid., p.66.
7. Ibid., p.135. See also James J. Hudson, *Hostile Skies: A Combat History of the American Air Service in World War I* (1968), p.94 (footnote).
8. Hudson, *op. cit.*, p.115 (footnote).
9. W. M. Fry, *Air of Battle* (1974), p.124.
10. Edwin C. Parsons, *I Flew with the Lafayette Escadrille* (1937, 1963), p.213.
11. The United States did not enter the First World War until April 1917, but before that a number of American volunteers flew with several units of the French *Corps d'Aviation*. On 20 April 1916 the French set up a special escadrille for American volunteers, the *Escadrille Américaine*. When, about six months later, the German ambassador to the United States protested against Americans fighting with the French, who in their communiqués mentioned an American escadrille, the name was abandoned. For a short time the escadrille's official number (N 124) was used only. Then Dr Edmund Gros — one of the leaders of the American Ambulance Service in France and later a major in the U.S. Air Service — suggested naming the escadrille after the

Marquis de Lafayette, French hero of the American Revolution. This caught on, and N 124 became the *Escadrille Lafayette*. (See Juliette Hennessy, "The Lafayette Escadrille — Past and Present", *Air Power Historian*, July 1957, pp.150-1).

12. Hudson, *op. cit.*, p.71.
13. Parsons, *op. cit.*, pp.322-3.
14. Duncan Grinnell-Milne, *Wind in the Wires* (1933), p.145 (of the 1968 Doubleday reissue).
15. Ibid., pp.196-8.
16. Sir Gordon Taylor, *Sopwith Scout 7309* (1968), pp.126-7.
17. Ernst Udet, *Mein Fliegerleben* (1935), pp.73-5.
18. Prof. Dr Johannes Werner, *Boelcke, der Mensch, der Flieger, der Führer der deutschen Jagdfliegerei* (1932), p.129. An English translation of this book was published in 1933, under the title *Knight of Germany*.
19. Immelmann, *op. cit.*, pp.152-3.
20. Spaight, *op. cit.*, pp.346-7.
21. Van Ishoven, *op. cit.*, p.70.
22. F. G. Nancarrow, *Glasgow's Fighter Squadron* (1942), p.38. The incident is also related in Guy Gibson, *Enemy Coast Ahead* (1946), pp.48-9.
23. Raymond F. Toliver & Trevor J. Constable, *Fighter Aces of the Luftwaffe* (1977), pp.94-5.
24. Quoted in Christopher Shores & Hans Ring, *Fighters over the Desert* (1969), p.223.
25. Quoted in Christopher Shores, Hans Ring & William N. Hess, *Fighters over Tunisia* (1975), p.398.
26. Anonymous, *Fighter Pilot; A Personal Record of the Campaign in France* (1941), pp.10-12. A post-war revised edition of this book (1955) revealed the name of the author: Wing Commander Paul Richey.
27. Toliver & Constable, *op. cit.*, pp.307-8..
28. Cajus Bekker, *Angriffshöhe 4000; Ein Kriegstagebuch der deutschen Luftwaffe* (1964), pp.82-3. An English translation of this book was published in the same year, under the title *The Luftwaffe War Diaries*.
29. Max Hastings, *Bomber Command* (1979), gives a detailed account of the Battle of the German Bight, on pp.22-35.
30. Toliver & Constable, *op. cit.*, p.179.
31. Ibid., p.190.
32. Ibid., pp.190-1, with a photograph of the party.
33. Ibid., pp.309/10. I have not been able to identify this RAF pilot. There is no mention of an American volunteer named Clarke in any of the records and lists I have available.

34. Bader's case was not unique. In the Second World War at least two other pilots flew on operations with two artificial legs. In Britain, Colin Hodgkinson served in 131, 501 and 611 Squadrons for nearly a year, flying Spitfires, before he crashed in occupied France on 23 November 1943 as a result of oxygen starvation, and was taken prisoner. (Colin Hodgkinson, *Best Foot Forward*, 1957). A Soviet fighter pilot, Alexei Maresyev, shot down seven German aircraft, flying with two artificial legs. He, too, survived the war. (*The Stars and Stripes*, April 25 1958).
35. Paul Brickhill, *Reach for the Sky: The Story of Douglas Bader* (1954), p.279. The other biography I have consulted is: Laddie Lucas, *Flying Colours: The Epic Story of Douglas Bader* (1981).
36. Brickhill, *op. cit.*, p.283.
37. Ibid., pp.290-1.
38. Ibid., p.291.
39. Adolf Galland, *Die Ersten und die Letzten* (1953), p.138.
40. Brickhill, *op. cit.*, pp.292-3.
41. Galland, *op. cit.*, p.138.
42. Brickhill, *op. cit.*, p.293.
43. Letter from Adolf Galland to the author, 7 March 1986.
44. Brickhill, *op. cit.*, pp.296-7.
45. Lucas, *op. cit.*, p.244.
46. Ibid., p.251.
47. This action is described in: Galland, *op. cit.*, pp.373-6, Jeffrey Ethell & Alfred Price, *The German Jets in Combat* (1979) p.55, and in Werner Held, *Adolf Galland: Ein Fliegerleben in Krieg und Frieden* (1983), pp.110 & 112.
48. Galland, *op. cit.*, p.140.
49. Interview with Adolf Galland, 12 November, 1985.
50. Toliver & Constable, *op. cit.*, p.113.

Chapter 7

1. Maurice Keen, *Chivalry* (1984), p.125.
2. Ibid. pp.132-3.
3. It is commonly thought that von Richthofen's planes were red all over, except for the national insignia of course. However, the rudder was often white and the undersurfaces light blue, as were those of the plane in which he met his death, the Fokker Dr I 425/17.
4. Richard Ward, *Sharkmouth* (Vol.1 *1916-1945*; Vol.2 *1945-1970*) (1970).
5. Quoted in Keen, *op. cit.*, p.30.

Chapter 8

1. As a matter of fact, the 1914-1918 war was not the first in which aircraft were used. This was done in the Italo-Turkish War, 1911-12, in Lybia. On 23 October 1911, Captain Carlos Piazza, commander of the Italian Air Flotilla, made the first war flight in history, a reconnaissance over the Turkish lines. Other activities followed: artillery observation, bombing and leaflet-dropping, but there was no air fighting, for the simple reason that the enemy had no aeroplanes. See the article by Flight-Lieutenant D. J. Fitzsimmons, *The Origins of Air Warfare*, in *Air Pictorial*, December 1972 issue.

2. As Huizinga says, "A direct line runs from the knight to the 'honnête homme' of the 17th century and the modern gentleman." (*Homo Ludens: A Study of the Play-Element in Culture*, p.104). An interesting side issue is whether women feel the same affinity to chivalry as men. Almost certainly they do not. Their attitude towards — and aptitude for — play greatly differ from those of men. They are even more different in their position on war and fighting in general. However, it is outside the scope of the present book to go into this further. Too little is known of the behaviour of women in aerial combat, or in any combat for that matter. The Soviet Union was the only country that used women pilots in combat roles, though more often than is generally known. In all, Soviet Air Force women pilots flew more than 24,000 sorties during the Second World War. (V. Hardesty, *Red Phoenix; The Rise of Soviet Air Power, 1941-1945*, 1982, p.193.).

3. Quoted in Huizinga, *op. cit.*, p.103.

Select Bibliography

Anonymous (Paul Richey) — *Fighter Pilot: A Personal Record of the Campaign in France* (B. T. Batsford 1941).

Bowyer, Chaz — *Albert Ball, VC* (William Kimber 1977).

Braham, Wing Commander J. R. D. "Bob" — *Scramble!* (Frederick Muller 1961).

Brickhill, Paul — *Reach for the Sky: The Story of Douglas Bader, DSO, DFC.* (Collins 1954).

Cole, Christopher — *McCudden VC* (William Kimber 1967).

Curry, Jack — *Lancaster Target* (Goodall Publications, © 1977).

Douglas, Sholto — *Years of Combat* (Collins 1963).

Douglas-Hamilton, Lord James — *The Air Battle for Malta: The Diaries of a Fighter Pilot* (Mainstream Publishing 1981).

Dudgeon, James M. — *'Mick': The Story of Major Edward Mannock, VC, DSO, MC* (Robert Hale 1981).

Fry, Wing Commander W. M. — *Air of Battle* (William Kimber 1974).

Funderburk, Thomas R. — *The Fighters: The Men and Machines of the First Air War* (Arthur Barker, © 1965, 1966).

Galland, Adolf — *Die Ersten und die Letzten* (Franz Schneekluth 1953).

Grinnell-Milne, Duncan — *Wind in the Wires* (Hurst & Blackett 1933).

Hardesty, V. — *Red Phoenix: The Rise of Soviet Air Power 1941-1945* (Arms and Armour Press 1982).

Hawker, Lieut.-Col. Tyrrel Mann — *Hawker, VC* (The Mitre Press/ Charles Skilton Ltd. n.d.).

Hodgkinson, Colin — *Best Foot Forward* (Odhams Press 1957).

Huizinga, Johan — *Homo Ludens: A Study of the Play-Element in Culture* (Originally published in Dutch, in 1938; © English translation: Roy Publishers 1950).

Immelmann, "Der Adler von Lille", herausgegeben von seinem Bruder. (v.Hase & Koehler 1934).

Ishoven, Armand van — *The Fall of an Eagle: The Life of Fighter Ace Ernst Udet* (© 1977; English version by Chaz Bowyer, William Kimber 1979).

Jones, Ira ("Taffy") — *Tiger Squadron: The Story of 74 Squadron R.A.F. in Two World Wars* (W. H. Allen 1954).

Keen, Maurice — *Chivalry* (Yale University Press 1984).

Kent, Group Captain J. A. — *One of the Few* (William Kimber 1971).

Lindbergh, Charles A. — *The Wartime Journals of* — (Harcourt Brace Jovanovich 1970).

McCudden, James Byford — *Flying Fury* (John Hamilton 1930).

'McScotch' — *Fighter Pilot* (Newnes 1936).

Mason, Jr, Herbert Molloy — *The Lafayette Escadrille* (Random House 1964).

Morris, Alan — *The Balloonatics* (Jarrolds 1970).

Parsons, Edwin C. — *I Flew with the Lafayette Escadrille* (E. C. Seale 1963).

Richthofen, Manfred Freiherr von — *Der rote Kampfflieger* (Im Deutschen Verlag 1933).

Rickenbacker, Captain Eddie V. — *Fighting the Flying Circus* (Doubleday 1965, © 1919).

Sims, Edward H. — *Fighter Tactics and Strategy 1914-1970* (Cassell 1972).

Taylor, Sir Gordon — *Sopwith Scout 7309* (Cassell 1968).

Toliver, Colonel Raymond F. & Trevor J. Constable — *Fighter Aces of the Luftwaffe* (Aero Publishers 1977).

Turner, Richard E. — *Mustang Pilot* (William Kimber 1970).

Udet, Ernst — *Mein Fliegerleben* (Im Deutschen Verlag 1935).

Werner, Prof. Dr Johannes — *Boelcke, der Mensch, der Flieger, der Führer der deutschen Jagdfliegerei* (v.Hase & Koehler 1932).